FREE

AFTER

SLAVERY

The Black Experience and The Freedmen's Bureau
in Reconstruction Texas

FREEDOM
AFTER
SLAVERY

The Black Experience and The Freedmen's Bureau
in Reconstruction Texas

LaVonne Jackson Leslie, Ph.D.

Order this book online at www.trafford.com
or email orders@trafford.com

Most Trafford titles are also available at major online book retailers.

Printed in the United States of America.

ISBN: 978-1-4120-5273-3 (sc)
ISBN: 978-1-4669-3008-7 (hc)
ISBN: 978-1-4669-3007-0 (e)

Library of Congress Control Number: 2012915687

Trafford rev. 02/06/2013

 www.trafford.com

North America & international
toll-free: 1 888 232 4444 (USA & Canada)
phone: 250 383 6864 ♦ fax: 812 355 4082

CONTENTS

Acknowledgements

My family inspired me to write <u>FREEDOM AFTER SLAVERY: The Black Experience and the Freedmen's Bureau in Reconstruction Texas</u>. Therefore, I would like to give thanks to my sisters, Glenda Turner, and Susie Lloyd, my brothers, Robert Chriesman and Lorenzo Chriesman II, my daughters, Christina Roberts, Angela Jackson, my son, Sharrod Perry, and grandson, Jadyn Jackson, and my dear nieces and nephews, and family members in Texas for their support. I dedicate this book to my dearly departed sister, Loretta Chappelle, who will always have a special place in my heart for believing in me, and loving me unconditionally. It was her encouragement that inspired me to achieve and to pursue my passion for history. I also want to thank my many friends. I really appreciate all the encouragement and support over the years.

I also gratefully acknowledge assistance from my editor. This project also would not have materialized without support from my colleagues. I give thanks to all supporting me in this endeavor.

CHAPTER 1

Overview of Reconstruction Studies on Texas

Freedom after slavery: The Black Experience and The Freedmen's Bureau in Reconstruction Texas, sheds information on the lives of African Americans in Texas, within the context of the black community and the family, with emphasis on the role of African American women, following the end of slavery during the Reconstruction period. My research revealed that many full-length studies on Reconstruction in Texas concentrated on the activities of African-American men more so than African-American women.[1]

Randolph Campbell's study, A Southern Community in Crisis: Harrison County, Texas, 1850-1880 (1983), provides useful information on economic conditions in Harrison County, Texas, during Reconstruction. Campbell places some emphasis on the black

---

[1]   Alwyn Barr, Reconstruction to Reform Texas Politics, 1876-1906 (Austin: University of Texas Press, 1971); Ira Berlin, et. al., eds., Freedom: A Documentary History of Emancipation: The Wartime Genesis of Free Labor: The Lower South (Cambridge, New York: Cambridge University Press, 1990); William E. B. DuBois, Black Reconstruction in America: An Essay Toward a History of the Part Which Black Folks Played in the Attempt to Reconstruct Democracy in America, 1860-1880 (New York: Atheneum Press, 1979); Peter Kolchin, First Freedom: The Responses of Alabama's Blacks to Emancipation and Reconstruction (Westport, Conn.: Greenwood Press, 1972).

family and economics. He provides insight on African Americans involvement in the economy, but mostly he gives information on agriculture in East Texas during and after slavery. He shows that during Reconstruction, the Freedmen's Bureau primarily assisted freedmen and freedwomen by urging them to be dedicated workers. He concludes that African-American women's participation in agricultural labor helped to sustain the African-American family.[2]

James Smallwood's <u>Time of Hope, Time of Despair: Black Texans During Reconstruction</u> (1981) discusses obstacles African Americans encountered during Reconstruction, with some emphasis on African-American women as wives and laborers. Smallwoood concentrates on counties in East Texas. He provides useful socioeconomic and cultural information on freedpeople in Texas during the period. Another historian, Lawrence Rice, in his work <u>The Negro in Texas, 1874-1900</u> (1971), provides useful information on freedpeople's economic, social, and political conditions in Texas during Reconstruction, with some emphasis on the significance of African-American women during the period.[3]

Barry Crouch provided an extensive collection of works on the African-American experience in Texas during Reconstruction. In his study, <u>The Freedmen's Bureau and Black Texans</u> (1992), he provides insight on the interactions of the Bureau with the black community. He examines how Bureau agents implemented policies concerning freedmen and women, and what effects their administration had upon the condition of the freedpeople. Crouch shows how the Bureau dealt with important topics such as labor and race relations in East Texas. Through a series of case studies on subdistricts in East Texas, that are

---

[2]   Randolph Campbell, <u>A Southern Community in Crisis: Harrison County, Texas, 1850-1880</u> (Baton Rouge: Louisiana State University Press, 1989), 300-303.

[3]   James Smallwood, <u>Time of Hope, Time of Despair: Black Texans During Reconstruction</u> (Port Washington: Kennikat Press, 1981), 43, 119; Lawrence Rice, <u>The Negro in Texas, 1874-1900</u> (Baton Rouge: Louisiana State University Press, 1971), 159-62.

representative of the Bureau's efforts, the author provides information on institutional, regional, individual, and social aspects of the Bureau.

Crouch also utilizes useful primary sources to provide information on the personalities of Bureau agents and their relations with freedmen and freedwomen. Crouch maintains that Bureau agents made concerted efforts to assist the African-American community. They also undertook efforts to protect African-American citizens encountering a hostile white community.[4]

In recent years, revisionist historians on Texas history have reconsidered developments during the Reconstruction period. These studies, however, consist of articles rather than full-length studies. A few of them, including Barry A. Crouch, Howard Beeth, and Cary D. Wintz, have written articles revealing information on the roles of freedwomen during Reconstruction in Texas. As a result, there is a significant need to have a more comprehensive book on Reconstruction in Texas, with freedwomen at the forefront, because questions still remain unanswered.

This book is significant in that it promises to provide answers on the history of freedwomen in East Texas during Reconstruction. This is important because as indicated by Barry A. Crouch, "contradictory perceptions surround the status and role of black women both in and out of bondage."[5] A more comprehensive study on freedwomen in Texas is needed to reflect their collective history, especially since as historian William Edward Burghardt Du Bois stated, African-American women's sacrifices produced "freedom and uplift" for themselves and their race.

Freedom After Slavery focuses on the geographical region classified as East Texas. It encompasses the area south of the Red River on the northern border and extending east of the Cross Timbers and Brazos

---

[4] Barry A. Crouch, The Freedmen's Bureau and Black Texans (Austin: University of Texas Press, 1992), 41-49.

[5] Barry A. Crouch, "Black Equality: Houston Black Women During Reconstruction," in Black Dixie: Essays on Afro-Texan History in Houston, ed. Howard Beeth and Cary Wintz (College Station: Texas A & M University Press, 1992), 54.

Rivers to the Arkansas and Louisiana borders (see Figure 1.1). It became known for its planter-dominated society and slavery; it housed some of the state's largest plantations. Slaves arrived to the area by slaveholders relocating from southern states during the Civil War in an effort to retain ownership of their slaves. After slavery ended, many former slaves remained in East Texas, most often because they had few options.[6]

The book uses information located in the Records of the Bureau of Refugees, Freedmen and Abandoned Lands (Freedmen's Bureau), oral interviews, and federal manuscript censuses. The records contain biographical and family information.

The Bureau records offer a window into the attitudes, aspirations, fears, and values of African-American people. In particular, they showed African-American women's concerns for family and children. Testimonies in the records indicate how African-American women actively dealt with issues and concerns affecting their lives and their families.

The records of the Bureau of the Census, located at the National Archives, make it possible to identify specific African-American females residing in Texas from 1865 to 1880. Also, these documents revealed the material conditions of freedwomen. The ninth census of the United States, 1870, and the tenth census of the United States, 1880, provide information on African-American household composition, the educational level of African-American females, the occupations of African-American females, and property ownership by African-American females.

The census data allow a demographic and economic profile of the African-American family and African-American women in East Texas. The data makes possible a concept of the communities' social structures by linking together information from population and agricultural

---

[6] Randolph B. Campbell, <u>An Empire For Slavery: The Peculiar Institution in Texas, 1821-1865</u> (Baton Rouge: Louisiana State University, 1989), 56-58.

schedules. There is a reasonably detailed view of the economic and social status of freedmen and freedwomen in the communities. The main samples for each year between 1865 to 1880 are limited to data on African-American heads of households and their dependents.[7]

The Ruth Winegarten Collection, in Special Collections at the Texas Woman's University Library, Denton, Texas, contains thirty-four folders of material on slavery and African-American women in Texas. The folders contain diaries and correspondence useful in documenting family and social aspects of African-American women lives following the Civil War. The material shows that African-American women labored with men in the fields and had similar economic restrictions imposed on them by former slaveholding planters. The planters documented freedwomen and freedmen's salaries which showed that many times African-Americans were cheated in terms of supplies, crops, and wages.[8]

The Records of Antebellum Southern Plantations from the Revolution through the Civil War, Series G, Part 1: Texas and Louisiana collections, edited by Kenneth Stampp, provide enlightening information on plantations in East Texas during slavery. These manuscripts illuminate family affairs. They provide information on the role of women. The records reflect upon racial attitudes, and the social and cultural lives of plantation owners who interacted with African-Americans during slavery in East Texas.[9] Although these records provoke scholarly interest on slaves, they fail to provide specific information on freedwomen during Reconstruction in Texas. The Rebecca McIntosh Hawkins Hagerty Papers, 1823-1901, Marion

---

[7] U.S. Bureau of the Census, Ninth Census (1870), Tenth Census (1880), Record Group 29, microfilm publication M-593, Washington, D. C.

[8] Texas Woman's University, Special Collections Archive, Ruthe Winegarten Collection, Texas Woman's University Library, Denton, Texas.

[9] Barker Texas History Center, Records of Antebellum Southern Plantations from the Revolution Throughout the Civil War, Part 1: Texas and Louisiana, Kenneth Stampp, ed., Records of Antebellum Southern Plantations from the Revolution through the Civil War, University of Texas, Austin, Texas.

and Harrison Counties, Texas, solicit information on freedwomen at the Phoenix Plantation near Marshall, Texas. The first series contains newspaper clippings describing the life of Rebecca Hagerty, the owner of the Refuge and Phoenix plantations in Marshall which employed many freedmen and freedwomen.[10] The Center for American History, Texas Archival Documents, located at the University of Texas at Austin, Natchez Trace Collection, contains the personal diaries and records of planter families.

Newspaper sources such as the Harrison Flag, the Texas Republican, and the Clarksville Standard report the attitudes of whites toward people during Reconstruction. These newspapers also contain information on the lives of the freedpeople, and at times make specific references to the experiences of women. Newspapers published by African-Americans in East Texas during the times report community issues, social and religious activities, and economic concerns of African-American women and men. Black newspapers include the People's Union and the Texas and Louisiana Watchman in Marshall; in Tyler, the East Texas Guard, and the Freeman's Press (also Freedmen's Press).[11]

Freedom and Family in Texas After Slavery draws upon secondary works on slavery, family history and women's studies to shed some information on freedwomen from slavery to emancipation. It utilizes Randolph Campbell's, An Empire for Slavery: The Peculiar Institution in Texas (1989), which focuses on slavery in Texas. According to Campbell, antebellum Texas depended on slave labor. The author's analysis of slavery includes information on slave women and the black family in East Texas.

---

[10] The University of Texas at Arlington, Special Collections Archives, Rebecca McIntosh Hawkins Hagerty Papers, 1823-1901, Marion and Harrison Counties, Texas, Arlington, Texas.

[11] Clarkville Standard (Clarkville), 5 April 1869; East Texas Guard (Tyler), 22 July 1908; Freeman's Press (also Freedman's Press) (Galveston), 25 August 1868; Harrison Flag (Marshall), 16 November 1867; People's Union (Marshall), 19 June 1904; Texas and Louisiana Watchman (Marshall), 15 March 1905; Texas Republican (Tyler), 16 June 1865.

The other studies on slavery did not specifically focus on slavery in Texas, however they provide intuitive information on the slavery period with emphasis on women. Although Jacqueline Jones's article, "'My Mother Was Much Of A Woman': Black Women, Work, and the Family Under Slavery," does not focus on slaves in Texas, it provides an argument in terms of male patriarchy and gender divisions, an important factor to consider when examining African-American female and labor during the slavery period. According to Jones, African-American women and men worked together and shared the obligations of family life during slavery. On another note, Jones argues that the more freedom the slaves had in determining their own activities the more clearly emerged a distinct division of labor between African-American women and African-American men. She concludes that values and customs within the slave community played a predominant role in structuring work patterns among slave households.[12]

Also focusing on race and gender during slavery, James Horton's "Freedom's Yoke: Gender Conventions Among Antebellum Free African-Americans," argues that race and gender affected antebellum free African-American women's roles. According to Horton, white society and African-American men expected African-American women to conform to certain standards based on their race and gender. Such standards hindered African-American women's abilities outside the domestic sphere. They were expected to be true women by taking care of the home and household work. In addition, African-American women were expected to work outside the home when necessary to provide for the economic good of the family.

Horton further maintains that free African-American women encountered the double burden of race and gender, which presented many difficulties in society. He maintains that they were responsible for uplifting the African-American race and setting good examples. Thus,

---

[12] Jacqueline Jones, "'My Mother Was Much of a Woman': Black Women, Work, and the Family Under Slavery," Feminist Studies 8 (Summer 1982): 253-55.

African-American women engaged in reform activities because of their sense of responsibility to improve conditions for African-American people. Horton concludes that African-American women gained political and economic importance expanding their role, but failed to eliminate traditional gender ideals restricting their status in society.[13]

Bert Loewenberg and Ruth Bogin, in Black Women in Nineteenth Century American Life: Their Words, Their Thoughts, Their Feelings (1976), maintain that emancipation symbolized for African-American women the opportunity to pursue goals, freedom to make decisions for their families, and the right to work at home or in the fields. Most important, Reconstruction meant freedom for many African-American women by allowing opportunities to make independent decisions concerning their concepts of womanhood and their personal lives.[14]

Dorothy Sterling in We Are Your Sisters: Black Women in the Nineteenth Century (1984), discusses the impact of emancipation upon the labor of African-American women. According to Sterling, throughout the South freedwomen attempted to assume feminine roles designated for white women who were regarded as being too delicate to labor outside the home. Sterling argues that African-American men encouraged African-American women to remain at home to take care of the family needs rather than labor in the fields or in the homes of former owners. The notions developed by African-American men about the proper role of African-American women as housewives served to shape their experiences according to gender. African-American women's sudden withdrawal from field labor indicates the first signal of differences between African-American males and females.

Many African-American women saw an opportunity for the first time to attend to the needs of their own families, but some expressed deep anger about the sacrifices they had to make. In many instances,

---

[13] James Horton, "Freedom's Yoke: Gender Conventions Among Antebellum Free Blacks," Feminist Studies 12 (Spring 1986): 51, 62-65.

[14] Bert Loewenberg and Ruth Bogin, Black Women in Nineteenth Century American Life: Their Words, Their Thoughts, Their Feelings (University Park: Pennsylvania State University Press, 1976), 14.

African-American women found themselves forced to give up thoughts of staying at home, so they worked in the fields alongside their husbands and children. African-American women who worked outside the home had to assume responsibility for maintaining their families because they were single parents or married women whose husbands worked in the fields.[15]

The widely accepted study on the African-American family by Herbert Gutman, The Black Family in Slavery and Freedom, 1750-1925 (1976), shows that among the first and perhaps the most important decisions that freedmen and freedwomen made was the reestablishment of family ties.[16] Even in a world where slavery no longer existed, African-American men and African-American women sustained the African-American family in the midst of economic and social obstacles, including lack of adequate housing, food, clothing, and health care. Gutman's use of Freedmen's Bureau Records and court documents proves that post-bellum apprenticeship laws in Texas entailed obstacles that made it difficult for African-American women to acquire custody of their children.[17]

Susan Mann's article, "Slavery, Sharecropping, and Sexual Inequality," maintains that African-American women's field labor diminished in sharecropping, because they devoted most of their attention to their families' needs in the household rather than to the needs of landowners. According to Mann, the decline in female field labor meant that in the African-American sharecropping household the sexual division of labor was more marked than in slavery. Furthermore, the author maintains that sharecropping families placed greater priority on women's role in household labor, which further reinforced a traditional sexual division of labor assigning women domestic roles. However in some instances African-American women switched roles and performed traditionally

---

[15] Dorothy Sterling, We Are Your Sisters: Black Women in the Nineteenth Century (New York: W. W. Norton, 1984), 321-27.

[16] Herbert Gutman, The Black Family in Slavery and Freedom, 1750-1925 (New York: Pantheon Books, 1976), 402.

[17] Ibid., 402-4.

male tasks as well as female household tasks.[18] In essence, this reflects African-American women's withdrawal from field labor with more emphasis on domestic duties within the household.

Claudia Goldin in "Female Labor Force Participation: The Origin of African-American and White Differences, 1870-1880," argues that race as opposed to class was a determining factor in African-American women's decisions regarding work during Reconstruction. In addition, the findings in Goldin's article showed that 20 percent of all African-American women worked as servants and that as many as 75 percent of those women lived in the homes of their white employer. Such findings merit further investigation to determine whether they were young, unmarried women, or mothers with children. In any case, Goldin's preliminary study introduces important themes in the history of Reconstruction African-American working women.[19]

Jacqueline Jones, Labor of Love, Labor of Sorrow: Black Women, Work, and the Family from Slavery to the Present, (1985), discusses the labor experiences of African-American women during slavery and Reconstruction. According to Jones, African-American women as freed laborers engaged in productive labor inside and outside their homes. African-American women considered kinship and work relations as a single economic unit, so first they were wives and mothers at home, and then laundresses and laborers outside the home. She concludes that this sometimes resulted in a few African-American women electing to stay at home to take care of their own families. Such women were primarily the wives and daughters of working men who supported the household. Those women who were sole supporters for their children or relatives assumed whatever employment they could locate. Jones's findings correspond with other works on African-American labor and

---

[18] Susan Mann, "Slavery, Sharecropping, and Sexual Inequality," Signs: Journal of Women in Culture and Society 14 (Summer 1989): 784.

[19] Claudia Goldin, "Female Labor Force Participation: The Origin of Black and White Differences, 1870-1880," Journal of Economic History 37 (March 1977): 96-98, 107.

freedwomen during Reconstruction by focusing on the withdrawal of freedwomen from wage labor as a major theme.[20]

Gerda Lerner, Black Women in White America: A Documentary History (1972), also introduces a well accepted theory on African-American women and labor. She maintains that African-American women during Reconstruction labored in the fields to enable their children to attend school rather follow their mothers into the fields. Lerner also shows that African-American women assumed household and domestic duties within the African-American family. African-American women educated their daughters to get them out of field work or domestic service and protected them from sexual harassment and white supervision.[21]

Noralee Frankel's dissertation, "Worker's, Wives, and Mothers: African-American Women in Mississippi, 1860-1870," concentrates on African-American women's lives and labor in the plantation south in a specific area during Reconstruction. Among other things, the study demonstrates the value of the Works Progress Administration's slave narrative collections, the official records of the Civil War, and National Archives records, in understanding the experiences of African-American women during Reconstruction. The study addresses questions and presents answers about the labor of slave women, the social experiences of African-American women during Reconstruction, and about the experiences of freed African-American women in other states.

According to Frankel, freedwomen both wanted and needed more time for their families. African-American women discovered that their domestic labor increased because many family chores were no longer performed communally as during slavery. They also disagreed with white employers over wage and contract issues because they needed decent pay to help take care of their families. Frankel concludes that

---

[20] Jacqueline Jones, <u>Labor of Love, Labor of Sorrow: Black Women, Work, and the Family from Slavery to the Present</u> (New York: Basic Books, Inc., 1985), 58-62.

[21] Gerda Lerner, ed., <u>Black Women in White America: A Documentary History</u> (New York: Random House Inc., 1972), 46, 158-59.

African-American women's primary concern for their families' welfare led them to support the demand for equal rights. She further shows that the choices of African-American women concerning their families and labor reflected the combined realities of gender, race, and poverty.[22]

Leslie Ann Schwalm's paper, "The Meaning of Freedom': African-American Women and Their Transition From Slavery to Freedom in Low Country South Carolina," provides useful information on field labor and domestic work performed by African-American women in low country South Carolina during Reconstruction. In field labor African-American women defended the task labor system, insisted on hourly wages, and rejected close supervision. This occurred because they wanted more control of their labor. It represented a unique situation because others did not use the task labor system.

Schwalm maintains that some African-American women supported themselves by performing field labor in their own fields.[23] In many instances, African-American women opposed restoration of confiscated lands to their former masters because it prevented them from acquiring such land. From a domestic labor standpoint, African-American women, Schwalm maintains, showed control over their labor by insisting domestic service be broken into tasks, and rejecting demeaning work, thus setting new boundaries on household labor. As a result of African-American women asserting more control over their labor, they had more time for their family needs. This discussion by Schwalm shows that African-American women responded to the articulation of gender used to shape labor policies. Also important, she points out that the Freedmen's Bureau used gender distinctions to shape labor policies used to separate African-American women from African-American

---

22 Noralee Frankel, "Workers, Wives, and Mothers: Black Women in Mississippi, 1860-1870," (Ph.d diss., George Washington University, 1983), 123-27.

23 Leslie Ann Schwalm, "'The Meaning of Freedom': African-American Women and Their Transition From Slavery to Freedom in Low Country South Carolina," Paper presented at the annual meeting of the Southern Historical Association, Atlanta, Georgia, 5 November 1992.

men.[24] In general, the trouble with this review of literature is that its generalizations do not necessarily hold in East Texas on an empirical basis. Overall, the sources provide necessary information useful in understanding slave women and freedwomen.

Freedom after slavery, consists of five topical sections that focus on the history of African-American women in East Texas during Reconstruction with emphasis on the black family. The first section deals with the transitional period from slavery to freedom. It places emphasis on the roles of women. It provides an overview of Texas history, slavery, slaveholders, and the black slave family. The second section deals with Reconstruction in Texas and focuses on the East Texas region. It places some emphasis on education in the black community. It provides background information on Freedmen's Bureau agents' roles in assisting the freedpeople. It defines the Freedmen's Bureau role in how they dealt with freedwomen. The next section examines Reconstruction and the black family with emphasis on freedwomen. It focuses on freedwomen's quest to locate family members, stabilize and legalize marriage, and child issues. The final section examines freedwomen and labor. It investigates freedwomen's occupations, labor contracts, and business ownership. Overall, the book maintains the assertive will of freedwomen, with the support of the Freedmen's Bureau in East Texas, aided the Black community and enabled the Black family to survive Reconstruction.

---

[24]   Ibid.

CHAPTER 2

The Transitional Period & Women:
Slavery Challenges

Jennie V. Parker's grandmother and great-grandmother were slaves in Clarksville, Texas in the 1850s when slavery was a fairly new institution. Parker's great-grandmother came to Texas as a slave from Alabama. She recalled when her grandmother, Jennie Allen, declared that "slaves in Texas never understood how slavery came about there, but they were glad when slavery was over and done with because those were some bad days." Jennie Parker also recalled the times her grandmother talked about how hard she worked on the cotton plantations for long hours.[25]

Although Jennie Allen was a child during slavery her account of bondage as related to Jennie Parker indicates that most slaves hated cotton plantation labor and often talked about running away. As a matter of fact, some slaves managed to escape slavery, but few were women. Those who remained on the plantations probably stayed because they did not want to leave their husband, children or other family members behind. But, many slaves escaped because as much as they understood it did not appear that slavery would ever end. So, regardless of whether

---

[25] Jennie V. Parker, Interview by Author, 14 November 1991, Ft. Worth, Texas, tape recording, Residence, Cisco, Texas.

slaves suffered abuse or received kind treatment, they sometimes realized they had to make decisions whether to accept their plight or to run away to gain freedom. Thus, according to Jennie Parker, in East Texas where her grandmother Jennie and great-grandmother lived, slaves desired freedom and risked their lives to escape slavery because it appeared firmly implanted. In their opinion, slaves hated the slavery.[26]

This section on slavery in East Texas primarily relies upon slave narratives to capture slaves interpretations of slavery. Historian Blassingame points out problems in terms of the reliability of the slave narratives, and with good reason. The slaves may have withheld information or distorted accounts of slavery during the interview because the interviewers were seldom black, thus they were fearful of giving straightforward information they thought might be used against them. This would be understandable because the interviews were collected in the 1930s during the period of Jim Crow and lynchings. To complicate matters, interviewers sometimes edited and revised the interviews before they were documented. To deal with this possibility, unedited versions of the interviews were examined. In essence, one has to use discretion when relying upon the material to portray slavery.

Therefore, secondary sources were also used to examine the black experience in Texas. The intent will be to determine how and why slaveholders intended to firmly implant slavery in Texas, and how slave men and women reacted to their status. To do this, it is necessary to start with the early history of slavery in Texas, specifically, how slavery evolved in East Texas.[27]

Texas represents one of the few slave states with only one comprehensive historical study on slavery, with the exception of Delaware. This is probably because Texas attempts to disassociate itself from its slave past by refusing to acknowledge itself as a southern state. It wants to be recognized as part of the Southwest with a frontier history.

---

[26] Ibid.

[27] John Blassingame, "Using the Testimony of Ex-Slaves: Approaches and Problems," Journal of Southern History 61 (1975): 81-87.

However, Texas joined the Confederacy in 1861 when it seceded from the Union and became part of the South. Thus, Texas inherited a legacy of slavery similar to other southern states. It's impossible to deny its slave history because slavery existed in the state. Furthermore, slavery was profitable in Texas as indicated by the slave narratives and historical works. These accounts show that slavery lasted in Texas, from 1820 until 1865, whereas in an original southern state such as Virginia it lasted from the mid-seventeenth century to the end of the Civil War.

Texas had only a small portion of the total slave population of the United States, less than 5 percent (based on the 1860 census), whereas, by comparison, Virginia had 12 percent and Louisiana had more than 8 percent. Also, Campbell maintains that slavery spread over only the eastern two-fifths of Texas before it was abolished in 1865. Slavery did not thrive as long in Texas as it did in older areas of the Antebellum South.[28] Therefore, except for the fact that Texas was newer as a slave state, it was essentially no different from the South. Politically, and economically, Texas functioned as part of the cotton kingdom South.

The evolution of the peculiar institution in Texas' history is quite unique. It goes back to the time when Mexico, the country Texas belonged to, gained its independence from Spain. Upon winning independence from Spain in 1821, Mexico began to encourage European immigrants to its Texas region north of the Rio Grande. Slavery as an institution in Texas came with white settlers during the 1820s. Stephen F. Austin and some other Americans from the lower Mississippi valley received grants for some of the best land in Texas. By 1830, about 30,000 Americans lived in Texas, far outnumbering the 4,000 Mexicans there. Looking forward to planting cotton, the American Texans had imported slaves by finding loopholes in Mexico's restrictions against slavery. The Mexican government, worried about

---

[28] Randolph B. Campbell, An Empire for Slavery: The Peculiar Institution in Texas, 1821-1865 (Baton Rouge: Louisiana State University Press, 1989), 2; U. S. Bureau of the Census, Population of the United States in 1860: Compiled from the Original Returns of the Eighth Census (Washington, D. C., 1864), ix, 193, 483, 515.

the strength of the American community in Texas, passed laws in 1830 that restricted American immigration and prohibited the importation of slaves.

These actions, and the news that American abolitionists planned to establish a refuge for free African-Americans in Texas, led American immigrants to begin violent protests. Protest turned to revolt after General Antonio Lopez de Santa Anna became President of Mexico. He thereafter appointed a military commander for Texas, and centralized power in Mexico City. A majority of Texans opposed Santa Anna's actions. In 1836, Texas forces under Sam Houston overthrew the Mexican government. On March 2, 1836, American Texans proclaimed their independence from Mexico and adopted a constitution legalizing slavery. Thus, once immigrant Texans gained their independence, they quickly gave slavery all the protection that it had never been granted by Mexican governments.[29]

One of the protections for slavery involved harsh constitutional and statutory restrictions on free blacks in Texas. Apparently, Texas imposed such restrictions on free blacks due to their fear that, although constituting only a small portion of Texas' population, they might threaten slavery, and cause rebellions.[30] However, no evidence supported such notions. Slaveholders also probably feared too many free blacks would inspire action for freedom. To prevent free blacks from encouraging such actions, state officials passed legislation to expel free blacks from the state. The Constitution of 1836 stated that free blacks could not reside in Texas without congressional authorization. This changed in 1837 when congress passed a joint resolution permitting all free blacks in Texas at the time of the declaration of independence to remain in the state.[31]

---

[29] T. R. Fehrenbach, <u>Lone Star: A History of Texas and the Texans</u> (New York: Macmillan Publishing Company, 1968), 146, 286-88; Campbell, <u>An Empire for Slavery</u>, 36.

[30] Campbell, <u>An Empire for Slavery</u>, 110, 113.

[31] Campbell, <u>An Empire for Slavery</u>, 110.

Another act in 1840 provided that after two years all "free persons of color" in Texas had to leave. All who remained after that time, without the permission of congress, could be sold as slaves. The law also prohibited free blacks from entering the state. Some free blacks such as the Ashworths, free blacks in Jefferson and Orange counties received special exemptions from both laws from President Sam Houston. They managed to acquire land and cattle, and even owned slaves. Of course, this was more unusual in Texas than in Louisiana, where many free blacks had large slaveholdings. The majority of free blacks remaining in Texas were subjected to the same harsh laws as slaves. For example, those accused of committing capital offense "crimes such as insurrection, poisoning, or rape of a white female," received the same punishment as slaves.[32]

Slave owners had good no reasons to fear free blacks because many of the slave insurrections of the 1850s did not involve them. The majority of the insurrections involved slaves themselves whose "objective in most Texas insurrections," was to escape to Mexico. In 1856, "Colorado County slaves, maybe as many as four hundred, plotted" to kill all the whites in the area and then go to Mexico. They armed themselves with knives and guns. However, the plot failed because a slave revealed it to the slave master. In Rusk, Harrison, and Red River Counties other plots were discovered and suppressed. The slaves involved in the plots were punished.[33]

Individual acts of violence against slavery occurred on a frequent basis. Slave women were involved in some of these acts. Lucy stayed in constant trouble with her master and mistress, so she killed her mistress. In 1858, Margaret, the twenty-one year old slave mistress to

---

[32] Randolph Campbell, An Empire for Slavery, 110; Hana Peter Nielson Gammel, comp., The Laws of Texas, 1822-1897, IV, 1115; I, 1292, 1385-86; II, 325-26, 468-69, 549-50, 789; Andrew F. Muir, "The Free Negro in Jefferson and Orange Counties, Texas," Journal of Negro History 35 (April 1950): 183-84, 195.

[33] Addington, "Slave Insurrections in Texas," 414-15, 417, 432; Campbell, An Empire for Slavery, 184.

Solomon Barrow of Liberty, used arsenic to kill him. It appears she did so because his will stated she would be manumitted upon his death and would receive $500 to move to a free state. In Fannin County, a female slave and two slave men, killed their master because they thought he had caused unrest among the slaves.[34]

Generally, in Texas, most slaves resisted slavery by running away alone or in small groups. Most runaways were young males, but there were incidents involving females. Sally Mae and Betty ran away together from their Robertson Count owner in 1860. Julie, a twenty-three year old slave, ran off to Clarksville to find a husband.

Another female slave, Sarah Allen did not have any desire to run away because her "missus would see her people had something good to eat every Sunday morning." According to Sarah, "you had to mind your missus and marster and you be treated well." Caroline Houston also did not run away because she thought she had a kind master.[35]

On another note, Texas' slave population increased faster than in other slave states. However, slavery did not grow into all areas of Texas at the same rate. The oldest area of major slaveholding was in Austin County, extending from the Gulf Coast inland along the Brazos and Colorado rivers in eastern Texas. Harrison, Bowie, and Red River counties in East Texas had approximately one-third of Texas' slaves during the 1840s. In 1850 Harrison and Bowie counties had a majority black population. Thereafter, the East Texas region around Nacogdoches and San Augustine northward through Harrison and Cass

[34] Galveston Weekly News, January 19, 1858 (Case of Solomon Barrow); January 5, 12, 19, 26, 1858 (Daugherty case); Addington, "Slave Insurrections in Texas," 420.
[35] Dallas Herald, December 19, 1860: Clarksville Northern Standard, December 26, 1857; Campbell, An Empire for Slavery, 182; Addington, "Slave Insurrections in Texas," 432; Rawick, The American Slave: A Composite Autobiography, Texas Narratives, Vol. 4, Part 1, 12 (Sarah Allen); Caroline Houston, File 4J295, Nacogdoches County, Works Progress Administration Records, Center for American History, Barker History Collection, University of Texas, Arlington.

counties, to the Red River border where Bowie, Red River, and Lamar counties joined, all continued to have a large number of slaves.[36]

These areas had large slave populations because slaveholding settlers had concentrated in these regions during the early settlement years. Most of the settlers were Southern planters who moved to Texas to acquire cheap or free lands, and brought their slaves with them. For many years, slaveholders had moved from the upper regions of the South. Approximately one half the white settlers migrated from Alabama and Tennessee. These settlers largely came from the hill and forest sections, not from the plantation South. They were yeomen farmers who settled into the prairie and post-oak regions far up the Texas rivers. On the other hand, the majority of immigrants to antebellum Texas migrated from the older southern states such as Virginia, Georgia, Mississippi, Tennessee or Alabama. Georgians settled into the pine woods in the northeast and established plantations. Georgians and Mississippians moved to the vicinity of Nacogdoches in east Texas. Tennesseeans went further west, across the two large prairies of north-central Texas, and to the edge of the cross timbers near Fort Worth. Many of these settlers brought with them their slaves and all aspects of slavery similar to their native states. Thus, slavery resembled a firmly established institution rather than one fairly new. It grew rapidly in the east Texas counties due to the type of agriculture in the areas, mainly cotton.[37]

By 1847, 100,000 white Texans owned slaves. Immigration into Texas was almost equally divided between the upper and the deep South, and the percentage of slaves, with the expansion of the cotton kingdom, consequently increased. As a matter of fact, more than one quarter of Texas families owned slaves during the 1850s. Slaves comprised approximately 30 percent of the state's total population in 1850. In 1850, Texas had 154,034 whites, 397 free blacks, and 58,161 slaves. Thus, slaveholders were determined to keep slavery intact because they

---

[36] Fehrenbach, Lone Star: A History of Texas and the Texans, 286-87; Campbell, An Empire for Slavery, 51, 57-58.

[37] Fehrenbach, Lone Star, 285-87.

had plenty to lose without slavery. Ten years later, in 1860, Texas had 182,000 slaves and 604,215 whites. The assessed value of all slaves was $106,688,920. Slaves did not live evenly throughout the settled areas of the state. They lived almost entirely on plantations in the eastern portion.[38]

Harrison County, the largest county in East Texas, served as the major cotton producing center in the Southwest. According to the census of 1850, the county's cotton production had increased 366 percent to 21,231 bales. This represented a substantial increase when compared to the 1849 production of 4,560 bales. Also, the county's production of corn increased from 377,902 bushels in 1849 to 647,732 bushels in 1859, thus ranking first in the state in both years. The county's slave labor produced 96 percent of the cotton in 1849 and 94 percent in 1859. They produced in corn production, 91 percent in 1849, and 88 percent in 1859. Female slaves accounted for two-thirds of the slave labor in cotton and corn production for both years.[39]

Similar to southern slave holding states, the vast majority of Texans did not own slaves, although they engaged in farming. In the census of 1860, 27 percent of the state's heads of households owned slaves. They controlled 73 percent of all wealth (real and personal property combined). More than half of the actual slaveholders owned five or less slaves. They supervised their own slaves, and frequently worked in the fields beside them. Although thousands of yeomen farmers owned between one to twenty slaves, the actual planting class was extremely small. It numbered about two thousand families. Of these, only fifty-four held one hundred or more slaves. Jerry Boykins' slave master owned 1,000 slaves. North Slades, a slave owner in Brownwood, had

---

[38] Fehrenbach, Lone Star, 289-90, 314; Campbell, An Empire for Slavery, 2; U.S. Bureau of the Census, Population of the United States in 1860, 483, 515.

[39] Randolph B. Campbell, "The Productivity of Slave Labor in East Texas: A Research Note," Louisiana %+39* 2 (1974): 158-60, 170-71; Seventh Census, 1850, Schedule 1,2, and,4, (Agriculture); Eighth Census, 1860, Schedule 1,2, and 4, (Agriculture).

former slave in Marshall, Texas

*Born in Slavery: Slave Narratives from the Federal Writers' Project,
1936-1938.* Slave Narratives, Federal Writers Project, Manuscript
Division, Library of Congress, Washington, DC.

an 1800 acre plantation. Since a good field hand could be rented out for $200 to $300 per year, or was expected to produce eight bales of cotton, these families were relatively rich. And since a healthy field hand cost as much as $2,000 in Texas, and a "plow boy" almost as much, the larger planters held an enormous money investment.[40]

Many planters had incomes of $5,000 or more while small farmers barely survived. The planter's prosperity allowed a life better than many in Texas. The Beverly Holcomb plantation at Marshall was one of the wealthiest in East Texas. Also, resulting from slave labor, the planter had time to be influential in state politics. Household heads owning slaves accounted for 68 percent of all federal, state, and local officeholders. The greatest planters were known throughout the state, and had some influence in Washington, the nation's capital.[41]

Most planters were male, however female owners were not uncommon. Females could own slaves due to an act passed January, 1840, by the Republic of Texas stating that land and slaves belonging to females at the time of marriage or received later as gifts or bequests would be considered "separate property of the wife." Furthermore, the state Constitution of 1845 provided that all property belonging to a woman before marriage or acquired thereafter "shall be her separate property." Based on these laws, women could maintain separate ownership of slaves throughout their married lives and, if they outlived their husbands, share in the common property accumulated during their marriage. Mary Avery from Cherokee County in East Texas provides a good example of Texas laws for female slaveholders. She owned a slave when she married James Avery in Georgia, but under the laws of that state, all property belonged to her husband. Under financial pressure, he sold her slave, and when his finances improved "following a move to Louisiana, he replaced the bondsman and gave Mary the bill of sale." The executor of his estate, Richard Avery, declared that Mary's

---

[40]   Rawick, ed., <u>The American Slave: A Composite Autobiography, Texas Narratives</u>, Part 1, Vol. 4, 121 (Boykins); 40 (Sarah Sanders).

[41]   Campbell, <u>An Empire for Slavery</u>, 210; T. R. Fehrenbach, <u>Lone Star</u>, 310-12.

slave belonged with the others claimed as common property, but Mary insisted that the slave belonged to her. The dispute reached the Texas Supreme Court, which ruled in 1854 that the slave belonged to Mary Avery. In another example, Rebecca McIntosh Hawkins Hagerty of Marion County survived two husbands and acquired ownership of 102 slaves in 1860.[42]

Female slaveholders treated slaves the same as male slaveholders. In some instances, both treated their slaves with dehumanizing indifference coupled with interest for their material welfare. Because it was easy for a slave to escape south of the Guadalupe or Colorado, slaveholders tried to keep them as contented as possible. Another reason, apparently, that slaves generally fared better in Texas than in some Southern states was that in Texas they were more valuable; they brought a greater price. These years saw a great "sale South" of surplus slaves from the Upper South, Virginia, Kentucky, and Missouri. However, they did not sell the older slaves. The history of slavery in America shows that where slaves were scarce, or in demand, they were treated with greater consideration.

---

[42] Hana Peter Nielson, comp., The Laws of Texas, 1822-1897, Vol. II, (Austin: Gammel Book Co., 1898-1902), 177-78, 1293; Randolph Campbell, An Empire for Slavery, 192.

Born in Slavery: Slave Narratives from the Federal Writers' Project, 1936-1938. Slave Narratives, Federal Writers Project, Manuscript Division, Library of Congress, Washington, DC.

CHAPTER 3

Transitional Period:
Slavery, Emancipation and the Black Family in Texas

The Black family faced many challenges during slavery, oftentimes due to abuse, neglect and separation. It wasn't unusual for slaves to live with their masters away from family members. Francis Black, a slave girl, was raised in the same house with her slave owners. According to Francis, they brought her clothes and took good care of her.[43] From another perspective, there were slave owners who mistreated their slaves. They often abused them by breeding and working them to death, or by separating them from their families.[44]

Slave owners sometimes bred their slaves without any regard to family relationship. They forced slave women to copulate with men. Annie Row remembered, like "the cows and the bull" women were bred for "bigger niggers." According to Jane Cotten, "We mostly were like cattle and hogs . . .". Other former slaves spoke of "breeding," "traveling," or "stud" blacks who in some cases went from one plantation to another to sire slave children. Fannie Brown said that although she

---

[43] Francis Black, File 4H357, Marshall, Texas, Works Progress Administration Records, Center for American History, Barker History Collection, University of Texas, Austin.

[44] Fehrenbach, Lone Star, 317.

had children before emancipation, "I never did have no special husban' 'fore the war."[45]

Some slave owners were "unwilling to breed" their slaves but intent to insure reproduction, forced "marriages" between slave men and women. Seventeen-year old Rose Williams did not understand what was expected when her master made her move from her parents' cabin to live with one of his male slaves. She resisted at first and refused to sleep with the man. Finally, however, she gave in due to threats from her master. Other slaves indicated that such "marriages" occurred. Betty Powers said, "Dem times cullud folks am jus' put together. De massa say, 'Jim and Nancy you go live together,' and when dat order give, it better be done." Lizzie Jones recalled that slaves weren't married by the "Good Book or the law." She further stated, "they jes' take up with each other and go up to the Big House and ask massa to let them marry." Then, "if they was ole enough, he'd say to the boy, 'Take her and go on home.'"[46]

Slaves had to obtain their masters permission to marry. Once they would obtain the master's permission, they would have a ceremony. The master of domestic servants either had the local white minister or the slave preacher perform the marriage ceremony. Couples had to jump over a broomstick together. According to Blassingame, the spouse "jumping over first, highest, or without falling was recognized by the wedding party as the one who would wear the pants or rule the family." Thus, jumping over the broomstick represented a significant aspect

---

[45] Campbell, <u>An Empire for Slavery</u>, 154-55; Rawick, ed., <u>The American Slave, Supplement</u>, (Westport, Conn.: Greenwood Publishing Co., 1979), Series 2, Vol. 8, 3369 (Annie Row), Vol. 3, 944 (Jane Cotton); Rawick, <u>The American Slave: A Composite Autobiography</u>, Part 1, Vol. 4, 155 (Fannie Brown).

[46] George P. Rawick, ed., <u>The American Slave, Supplement</u>, Series 2, Vol. 10, 4121-23 (Rose Williams); <u>The American Slave: A Composite Autobiography</u>, Part 3, Vol. 5, 191 (Betty Powers); Part 2, Vol. 4, 246 (Lizzie Jones).

Francis Black

Born in Slavery: Slave Narratives from the Federal Writers' Project, 1936-1938. Slave Narratives, Federal Writers Project, Manuscript Division, Library of Congress, Washington, DC.

Betty Powers

*Born in Slavery: Slave Narratives from the Federal Writers' Project,
1936-1938. Slave Narratives, Federal Writers Project, Manuscript
Division, Library of Congress, Washington, DC.*

of the marriage ceremony. Molly Dawson recollected the pre—and post-nuptial festivities when she married.[47]

Slaves often had cross-plantation marriages. Many slave men did not want a wife from the same plantation. This way, they did not have to watch slave masters abuse their wives without providing some protection. Spouses, however, who lived on separate plantations saw each other less frequently than those who lived on the same plantations. Slave owners seldom interfered with a slave's selection of a mate unless the future spouse lived on another plantation. They often encouraged slave marriages because they felt that they would result in a more stable work force with less runaways because slaves did not run away as much once they had a family. Most often, slave owners preferred having their slaves marry on their own plantations. According to Will Adams, his master did not like his slaves to "to marry off the place." They knew they could not benefit from the marriage if the slave wife did not live with her spouse because they would have no control over her labor or the children since they lived their mother. In some cases, wealthy slave owners tried to buy the woman whom his male slave wanted to marry. In this way, the slave owner acquired the labor of the woman and the couple's children. Hattie Cole, Martha Spence Bruton, and Gill Ruffin all remembered their fathers being brought from other masters in order to unite them with their spouses and children.[48]

Most masters, however, decided not to "breed" or "force marriages." Instead, they allowed slaves to form families and assume responsibility for bearing and rearing children. In some cases, a woman and her

---

[47] Rawick, <u>American Slave, Supplement</u>, Series 2, Vol. 2, 174 (Joe Barnes); Vol. 3, 709 (Jeptha Choice), Vol. 4, 1132 (Mollie Dawson); Vol. 6, 2298 (Lu Lee); Blassingame, <u>The Slave Community</u>, 166.

[48] Rawick, <u>The American Slave: Texas Narratives</u>, Part 1, Vol. 4, 3 (Will Adams); <u>American Slave, Supplement</u>, Series 2, Vol. 3, 776 (Hattie Cole); Vol. 9, 3493-94 (George Sells); Vol. 3, 521 (Martha S. Bruton); Vol. 8, 3376 (Gill Ruffin); Noralee Frankel, "Workers, Wives, and Mothers: Black Women in Mississippi, 1860-1870" (Ph.D. diss., George Washington University, 1983), 145-46; Blassingame, <u>The Slave Community</u>, 164-65.

Fanny Brown

Born in Slavery: Slave Narratives from the Federal Writers' Project, 1936-1938. Slave Narratives, Federal Writers Project, Manuscript Division, Library of Congress, Washington, DC.

children were referred to as a family. Eda Rains's mother finally had the opportunity to raise Eda and her brothers. According to Eda, they "had their own cabin." Emma Taylor and her three brothers, along with three sisters, lived with their mother. She did the cooking for the whole family.[49] Thus, the "female-headed" family "existed during slavery." However, a man, his wife, and their children constituted the typical slave family as identified by "slave holders and slaves alike."[50] Texas slave narratives reveal that nuclear slave families existed. Using a sample of 181 narratives, Campbell maintains that "60 percent remembered living with both parents on the same" plantation "and another 9 percent recalled that their fathers lived nearby on a neighboring farm or plantation."[51]

Slave owners probably realized the importance of permitting and encouraging their slaves to live in nuclear families. They recognized the importance of kinship ties and how determined slaves were to sustain them. They could see that such unions resulted in children as well as ties and obligations that made their slaves more controllable. Family ties also provided slaves with love. In late 1862, Fannie, a slave woman, wrote to her husband Norflet while he served his master in the Confederate Army, from "Spring Hill" plantation in Harrison County, Texas. Fannie expressed concern over whether they would be rejoined. She lovingly wrote, "I haven't forgot you nor I never will forget you as long as the world stands, even if you forget me . . . no knife can cut our love into [sic]." She expressed greetings from "Mother, Father, Grandmama, Brother & Sisters." They all hoped Norflet would "do well." This letter reflected strong family ties.[52]

---

49 Rawick, ed, The American Slave: A Composite Autobiography, Part 3, Vol. 5, 225 (Eda Rains); Eda Raines, 4J295, Cherokee County; Emma Taylor, FJ295, Tyler, Texas, Works Progress Administration Records, Center for American History, Barker History Collection, University of Texas, Austin.

50 Campbell, An Empire for Slavery, 156.

51 Ibid., 156.

52 Randolph B. Campbell and Donald K. Pickens, eds., "'My Dear Husband': A Texas Slave's Love Letter, 1862," Journal of Negro History, 65 (Fall 1980): 361-64; Campbell, An Empire for Slavery, 157-59.

Will Adams

Born in Slavery: Slave Narratives from the Federal Writers' Project, 1936-1938. Slave Narratives, Federal Writers Project, Manuscript Division, Library of Congress, Washington, DC.

Despite the fact slave owners occasionally allowed slaves to maintain families, they were not totally happy because their enslaved status deprived them of basic human rights. Slaves in the quarters viewed slavery different than whites because they suffered in other ways. When one examines the slave community in East Texas, the institution had definite disadvantages for slaves. Their quarters were often inadequate. On the plantation where Katie Darling lived, slaves lived in one-room log houses that had two bunks to the house, and they slept on straw mattresses.[53]

As slaves, black men could no longer exercise the same power over their families as they had in Africa. The transformation of African familial roles led to the creation of America's first democratic family in the quarters, where men and women shared authority and responsibility. The husband demonstrated his importance in the family unit by providing food, clothing, and other basic supplies provided by slave owners. They often hired themselves out, and hunted and fished to provide additional food. The wife took care of the children and prepared food for the family.[54]

Plantation labor probably hindered the amount of care and love slave parents could give their children. On many plantations the women did not have enough time to prepare meals and were generally too exhausted to cook after working in the cotton fields. However, they managed to do the best they could with what they had. Slave children often received attention and love from both parents despite lack of adequate food and shelter. Mothers spent their spare time with their children. Fathers who lived on other plantations made regular visits to spend time with their wives and children. Laura Rays's father lived on another plantation, but, he would always come back to see her, and he would help to sell the cotton in the Fall. Martha Spence

53 Katie Darling, File 4H357, Marshall, Texas, Works Progress Administration Records, Center for American History, Barker History Collection, University of Texas, Austin.

54 Rawick, <u>American Slave, Supplement</u>, Series 2, Vol. 6, 2402 (Sue Lockridge); Vol. 7, 2602-2603, 2607 (Louise Matthews); Blassingame, <u>The Slave Community</u>, 178-79.

Bunton's reunited with her father when her mother died with diptheria. As a result of her mother's death, her "pappy had to be mammy and pappy."[55] Generally, slaves who provided for their families gained status in the slave quarters.[56]

Slave women took initiatives to help their children cope with slavery. They encouraged them to have faith that God would end slavery. Most importantly, slave mothers taught their children to be honest. As a child, Liza Jones' mother used to sing a song with the lyrics, "don't steal," and another one telling her to trust God. Millie Ann Smith in Rusk County, remembers the times she prayed with her mother. She stated, "I 'member mammy used to sing like this:"

> "Am I born to die, to lay this body down,
> must my tremblin' spirit fly into worlds
> unknown, The lands of deepes' shade,
> Only pierce' by human thought.'" [57]

Slave children who did not obey their slave parents often received punishment. Molly Dawson recalled that children "who misbehaved got a good spanking." Mandy Morrow received a spanking from her mother when she sneaked away to smoke a pipe.[58]

Slave children did not like to be separated from their mothers. Willis Easter caused so much trouble without his mother until his master had to send for her to come and live with him. Eda Raines, a slave child,

[55] Laura Ray, File 4J295, Cherokee County, Texas, Works Progress Administration Records, Center for American History, Barker History Collection, University of Texas, Austin; Rawick, The American Slave: A Composite Autobiography, Part 2, Vol. 4, 174 (Martha Spence Bun)

[56] John Blassingame, The Slave Community: Plantation Life in the Antebellum South (New York: Oxford University Press, 1979), 179-81.

[57] Rawick, ed., The American Slave: A Composite Autobiography, Part 2, Vol. 4, 242-243 (Liza Jones); Part 4, Vol. 16, 43 (Millie Ann Smith); Blassingame, The Slave Community, 183, 187-90.

[58] Rawick, ed., American Slave, Supplement, Series 2, Vol. 2, 1125-26 (Molly Dawson); Vol. 7, 2775-76 (Mandy Morrow).

did not like the fact that she was hired out away from her mother. According when she was hired out to the Tomlin family at Douglass she got really lonesome, "for she was just a little girl who wanted to see her mother." Ella Washington cried and pleaded with her master to not separate her from her mother and sister. According to Ella, "us all cryin hard, cause us thunk [thought] us gwine git sep'rate [separated]." The master decided to keep them together.[59]

Overall, kinship ties with children, husbands, and family members remained significant in the slave community. They served as important survival mechanisms for slaves. This enabled them to endure because they faced overwhelming obstacles in their efforts to survive and build strong stable families. First, the master restricted their authority. Any decisions slaves made regarding their families tended to be countermanded by their masters. Slave masters determined when both he and his wife would go to work, when or whether his wife cooked his meals, and often intervened in family disputes. In enforcing discipline, masters would whip both husband and wife when they had loud arguments or fights. Some masters punished males by refusing to allow them to visit their mates on other plantations. Under such restraints, slave fathers often had little or no authority over family issues. To make matters worse, black males frequently could do little to protect their wives from the sexual advances of whites. In many instances, the women had to submit.[60] Moreover, slave women and men had to cope with family concerns, and meet labor demands imposed upon them by their masters.

In terms of labor, the majority of Texas slaves worked on farms and small plantations. Slave men, women, and children often worked together in the fields. Virtually all slaves in East Texas worked as cotton pickers. Sarah Ashley picked as much as 300 pounds of cotton, and

---

[59] Rawick, ed., The American Slave: Texas Narratives, Part 2, Vol. 4, 1 (Easter), Part. 4, Vol. 16, 132 (Washington); Aunt Eda Rains, File 4J295, Cherokee County, Works Progress Administration Records, Center for American History, Barker History Collection, University of Texas, Austin; Blassingame, The Slave Community, 191.

[60] Blassingame, The Slave Community, 172.

carried "it a mile to" the cotton house. Some of the other slaves gathered anywhere from 300 to 800 pounds of cotton.[61]

The field hands usually worked from sun up to night time. Sarah Sanders recalls that the work day started at 5:00 a. m. and lasted until sundown. In the field, the men did the heaviest work, such as plowing, chopping trees, and ditching. The women sowed corn and cotton seed, and labored as hoe hands. They worked so late into the night that cotton had to be weighed in by candlelight. At night the men had to shuck corn and the women would "card and spin." The children also had chores. They worked from an early age performing jobs like carrying water, gathering firewood, and knocking down old cotton stalks. As a young child, the first work Emma Taylor ever did was helping to feed the chickens and the geese. She had to feed them every morning and every night, and during the day, she had to help "shell the corn off the cobs to feed them with." Once the children got older, they would tend livestock. However, most began to do some field work by the time they reached their teens. When Emma got older, she worked all day picking and chopping cotton, or hoeing corn.[62]

A few female slaves who lived on farms and plantations did not work in the fields. In some instances, they worked as cooks, laundresess and ironers, seamstresses, and spinners and weavers. Amy Else's mother, named Lucy, worked as a cook and spinner. Most slaveholders had female slave cooks, and some larger plantations employed one for the owner's family, one for the overseer who supervised the slaves, and one or more for the slaves. Many of the women who worked as spinners and weavers did so at night after working in the fields all day, although some spinned and weaved for their masters on a full time

---

[61] Rawick, ed., The American Slave, Part 1, Vol. 4, 35 (Sarah Ashley).

[62] Katie Darling, File 4H357, Marshall, Texas; Emma Taylor, 4J295, Tyler, Texas, Works Progress Administration Records, Center for American History, Barker History Collection, University of Texas, Austin; Abigail Curlee, "A Study of Texas Slave Plantations, 1822-1865" (Ph.D. diss., University of Texas, 1932), 205-11; Rawick, American Slave, Supplement, Series 2, Vol. 2, 408 (Jacob Branch); American Slave: A Composite Autobiography, Series 1, Vol. 4, 39 (Sarah Sanders).

basis. According to freedwoman Laura Ray, the women would "knit and spin at night and at odd times. Aunt Tob was the spinner and Aunt Narciss the weaver." Laura Cornish, for example, remembered that her mother "was the seamstress and don't do nothing but weave cloth . . . and make clothes."[63]

A few slaves in East Texas, not owned by farmers or planters, lived in towns such as Marshall. Most of the women labored as domestic servants. A few women worked in factories. In 1858, Henry Ware of Glade Springs in Harrison County, had a factory where slave women made linsey jeans, blankets, yarns, and russet shoes. Men worked in a variety of jobs as laborers and skilled craftsmen. Town slaves had better work conditions than farm or field slaves. Amy Else's father worked as a skilled carpenter. According to Amy, her father had not worked hard. Also important, the living conditions in town sometimes appeared to be much better for skilled slaves and their families. Based on Amy's account, the "quarters" in town were good houses, with beds and bed clothes.[64]

In many instances, slaves endured harsh working conditions whether they lived on rural plantations or in towns. They often suffered due to heavy work and long work hours. It appears that slave owners only allowed slaves to have Saturday afternoons and Sundays as free time, therefore slave women could not dedicate as much time to family needs as they desired. On the plantation where Harriet Chesley lived, the slaves had a church they attended every Sunday. They did not work on Saturday evening, but the "women folks washed and then ironed on

---

[63] Laura Ray, File 4J295, Cherokee County; Amy Else, File 4H357, Marshall, Texas, Works Progress Administration Records, Center for American History, Barker History Collection, University of Texas, Austin; Clarksville, Northern Standard, February 3, 1855, March 1, 1856, August 17, 1861; John Michael Vlach, "Afro-American Folk Crafts in Nineteenth Century Texas," Western Folklore 50 (1981), 151-55; Rawick, The American Slave, Supplement, Series 2, Vol. 7, 2516 (C. B. Mc Ray), Vol. 3, 937 (Laura Cornish); Campbell, An Empire for Slavery, 122-23.

[64] Amy Else, File 4H357, Marshall, Texas, Works Progress Administration Records, Center for American History, Barker History Collection, University of Texas, Austin; Texas Republican (Marshall), May 15, September 17, 1858; Campbell, An Empire for Slavery, 125.

Saturday night." They would rest on Sunday evening.[65] Although slaves may have had free time from work, they still had to deal with harsh constraints imposed upon them by slave owners.

The institution of slavery in east Texas did not change until the period of the Civil War. It gradually changed when Texas joined the Confederacy. Most East Texans supported secession. In thirty of the thirty-five east Texas counties from Red River County through Leon County on down to Galveston counties on the coast, over seventy-five percent of the voters approved secession. In many East Texas counties the vote for secession was overwhelming; in Anderson, Harrison, Newton, Polk, Panola, Smith, Trinity, and Tyler counties over ninety-percent of the voters endorsed secession. Nevertheless, their efforts proved futile as they lost the Civil War, and their slaves were emancipated.[66]

Freedom did not come to Texas slaves until June 19, 1865, when Gordon Granger, the General Commander of the District of Texas, arrived in Galveston to enforce the Emancipation Proclamation. It provided for the abolition of slavery. As a result of the proclamation, Granger issued General Order Number Three, which stated "all slaves are free." This act initiated Texas Reconstruction. According to historian Eric Foner, "Reconstruction allowed the scope for a remarkable political and social mobilization of the black community . . . for a moment, American freedmen had enjoyed an unparalled opportunity to help shape their own destiny."[67]

---

[65]   Harriet Chesley, 4H357, Harrison County, Works Progress Administration Records, Center for American History, Barker History Collection, University of Texas, Austin.

[66]   Ralph A. and Robert Wooster, "A People at War: East Texans during the Civil War," East Texas Historical Journal 28 (January 1990): 4-5.

[67]   Diane Neal and Thomas W. Kremm, "'What Shall We Do With The Negro?', The Freedmen's Bureau in Texas," East Texas Historical Journal 27 (1989): 23; James Marten, Texas Divided: Loyalty and Dissent in the Lone Star State, 1865-1874 (Lexington: The University Press of Kentucky, 1990), 155; Randolph P. Campbell, A Southern Community in Crisis: Harrison County, Texas, 1850-1880 (Austin: Texas State Historical Association, 1983), 17; Eric Foner, Nothing But Freedom: Emancipation and Its Legacy (Baton Rouge: Louisiana University Press,

Upon hearing the news of freedom approximately 200,000 freedpeople in Texas, a large percentage of them freedwomen, remained on plantations in East Texas[68].

Lizzie Hughes and her husband moved to Harrison County near Marshall. She and her husband farmed, and she "cooked and kept' house for the white folks round town." She saved her money which enabled them to purchase their own farm.[69] Richard Jackson's parents immediately left their former owners, the Rosboroughs, upon emancipation and moved to a farm near Woodlawn.[70] Ellen Payne, an ex-slave of Texas Governor E. B. Clark and pioneer physician Dr. Charles Evans, ignored her mistress's pleas to stay with them. Instead, she left with her mother and Nelson Payne, and relocated to a farm in Marshall.[71]

Most of the freedpeople encountered freedom without any belongings. Slaves such as Minerva Bendy had masters who turned them loose in the woods to face hard times. They did not know what to do when former masters made them leave the plantations. Freedom was new, and Minerva did not know where to turn because she "wasn't raised to do nothin." Furthermore, her former master "didn't even give them a hoecake or a slice of bacon." So, they had to deal with freedom the best way they could, and they did this by going where they could survive. Susan Ross's oldest brother left the plantation to improve his

1983), 72-73. These secondary sources provide interesting information on freedpeople during Reconstruction emphasizing social and political dynamics in the African-American community.

[68] Charles E. Tatum, <u>Mount Zion: In The Shadow Of a Mighty Rock, Centennial Edition, 1877-1977</u> (Houston: C. Edwards and Associates, 1977), 9.

[69] Lizzie Hughes, File 4H357, Marshall, Texas, Works Progress Administration Records, Center for American History, Barker History Collection, University of Texas, Austin.

[70] Richard Jackson, File 4H357, Marshall, Texas, Works Progress Administration Records, Center for American History, Barker History Collection, University of Texas, Austin.

[71] Ellen Payne, File 4H357, Marshall, Texas, Works Progress Administration Records, Center for American History, Barker History Collection, University of Texas, Austin.

Born in Slavery: Slave Narratives from the Federal Writers' Project, 1936-1938. Slave Narratives, Federal Writers Project, Manuscript Division, Library of Congress, Washington, DC.

condition. He quickly left without taking time to gather his material belongings because he could not wait to expand his horizons. Upon hearing the news that he was free, he gave a whoop, ran and jumped a fence, then told his mother and sister good-bye. When asked where her brother went, Susan responded, "I don't know where he go, but I never did see him again."[72]

Many ex-slaves left the plantations without any notice to their former slave masters because they feared that they would be forced to stay. In spite of their efforts to experience freedom, many ex-slaves failed to escape from their former master's plantations. Therefore, not all of them experienced the joy of leaving their former masters since many former slave masters had made it known that they would not give them their freedom. Prominent former slave owners often attempted to stop ex-slaves from claiming their freedom by denouncing the Reconstruction laws, stating that "the people would be justified in opposing them" in order to keep their former slaves from leaving. To further show their opposition to emancipation, some whites assaulted freedpeople. Susan Merritt from East Texas recounted how freedpeople in Rusk County were killed rather than freed. When they attempted to escape into Harrison, "they owners have 'em bushwhacked . . . you could see lots of . . . hangin' to trees in Sabine bottom right after freedom', cause they cotch 'em swimmim' cross Sabine River and shoot 'em."[73] According to Annie Row, who also lived in Rusk County, "master starts cussin' de war and him picks up de hot poker and say 'Free de . . . , well dey? I free dem." Then, he hit Annie's mother in the neck with the poker, and "takes de gun offen de rack and starts for de field whar de . . . am a workin." Fortunately for the slaves, he collapsed before he reached the field and died the following day.[74]

As the news of freedom spread, slaveowners continued to refuse to give up their slaves. Mariah Snyder's former master kept her three years

---

[72] Rawick, The American Slave: Texas Narratives, Part 1, Vol. 4, 69 (Minerva Bendy); Supplement 2, Vol. 4, Part 3, 1103-4 (Susan Ross).

[73] Smallwood, Time of Hope, Time of Despair, 34

[74] Marten, Texas Divided: Loyalty and Dissent, 167.

after Emancipation. Dinah Watson's former owners refused to give her to her parents upon the news of freedom, and kept her two years.[75] According to historian James Smallwood, former masters adamantly refused to free freedpeople because they still wanted to control their lives. Furthermore, he asserts that former owners informed freedpeople of the Emancipation only after rumors of freedom became so strong that they could not be denied, and some tried to trick them into staying until they had produced the summers' crops.[76] Tempie Cummins's mother, a cook, overheard her former master state the slaves were unaware that they were free, so he was "going to wait to tell them after they had made another crop or two." She went to the fields and told the other slaves. They all quit at once when they realized they had their freedom. Shortly thereafter, Tempie's mother went back to her former master's plantation to make her final escape and take Tempie with her. Her former master tried to stop her mother from leaving by shooting at her and Tempie. Nevertheless, they managed to escape.[77]

Oftentimes, slaves learned about their freedom when socializing with each other.[78] According to Lizzie Jones in Harrison County, "The white folks didn' let them know that they were free until almost a year after the war. Massa Hargrove, she states, "took sick sev'ral months after and 'before he did, he told the white folks not to let us go unless they have to. Finally the slaves found out they had been freed, so they departed." Susan Merritt in Harrison County heard about freedom in September while she was picking cotton in the field. A freedmen's

---

[75]   Mariah Snyder, File 4H357; Dinah Watson, Marshall, Texas, Works Progress Administration Records, Center for American History, Barker History Collection, University of Texas, Austin.

[76]   Smallwood, Time of Hope, Time of Despair, 33-34.

[77]   Rawick, ed., The American Slave, Part 1, Vol. 4, 264 (Tempie Cummins); Ronnie C. Tyler, The Slave Narratives of Texas (Austin: Encino Press, 125; Lamar L. Kirven, "A Century of Warfare: Black Texans," (Ph.D. diss., Indiana University, 1974), 4.

[78]   Jeanne Noble, Beautiful Also Are the Souls of My Black Sisters: A History of the Black Woman in America (Englewood Cliffs: Prentice-Hall Inc., 1978), 56; B. A. Botkin, Lay My Burden Down: A Folk History of Slavery (Chicago: University of Chicago Press, 1945), 45.

bureau agent came by and told her master that he had to free his slaves. Isabella Boyd recalled that "it was a long time before I'se know I was free because the master wanted to get through with the corn and cotton crops." After she was notified by freedpeople from another plantation that she was no longer a slave, she was still forced to stay and work for her former master.[79]

Further evidence shows that many freedwomen in East Texas created elaborate plans to flee from their former masters after they had heard about their freedom. Annie Osborne, a freedwoman in Marshall, escaped when her master refused to let her and her mother go after the provost marshal had told him to free them. According to Annie, her mother planned the escape. She stated, "my mammy pretends to go to town and takes my brother, Frank and goes to Mansfield and asks the Progoe [Provost] Marshal what to do. He say we's free as old man Tom and didn't have to stay no more. Frank stays in town and mammy brings a paper from the progoe [Provost], but she's scared to give it to Massa Tom. Me and James out in the yard makin' soap. I's totin' water from the spring and James fetchin' firewood to put round the pot. Mammy tells James to keep goin' next time he goes after wood and her and me come round another way and meets him down the road. That how we got "way from old man Bias." Katie Darling escaped from her former master's plantation with the assistance of her brother.[80]

For some African-American women, changing plantations to gain freedom was as exhausting psychologically as it was physically because they suspected it would be difficult to find employment and housing.

---

[79] Rawick, ed., The American Slave, Part 2, Vol. 4, 248 (Lizzie Jones); Part 3, Vol. 5, 75 (Susan Merritt); Part 1, Vol. 4, 115 (Isabella Boyd); Isabella Boyd, File 4H357, Marshall, Texas, Works Progress Administration Records, Center for American History, Barker History Collection, University of Texas, Austin.

[80] Rawick, ed., The American Slave, Part 3, Vol. 5, 158-59 (Annie Osborne); Katie Darling, File 4H357, Works Progress Administration Records, Center for American History, Barker History Collection, University of Texas, Austin; Rawick, ed., The American Slave, Part 1, Vol. 4, 280 (Katie Darling).

Susan Merritt

Born in Slavery: Slave Narratives from the Federal Writers' Project, 1936-1938. Slave Narratives, Federal Writers Project, Manuscript Division, Library of Congress, Washington, DC.

Hannah Scott wondered what she "gwine [going] to do" upon freedom. She also recalled witnessing lots of freedpeople "not doin' so well as they did when they was slaves and not havi'[having] nigh as much to eat." Therefore, some freedpeople decided to stay in familiar surroundings rather than face others they did not know. For example, Mattie Gilmore's stepmother stayed and cooked for her former master four or five years after emancipation.[81] In Cherokee County, Laura Ray's "mother and us chillun stayed on thar for several years" because they had no other place to go to.[82] According to Emma Taylor in Tyler, "nearly all stayed on the lantation [plantation] for a long time."[83] Nancy King told how "Old Missie freed us but said we had a home as long as she did. Me and my husband' stays 'bout a year . . . ." They probably stayed because they knew at least they would have some food and shelter, rather than face the uncertain.[84] Jordan Smith's mother stayed with her former master, however she refused to let her son stay with her. Jordan left to live with his uncles and aunts.[85] Apparently, they all elected to stay with their former masters just to have a means of support.

Freedpeople may have remained with former slave masters for reasons other than insecurity about how to make a living; some probably stayed with their former masters for protection from white supremacy groups such as the Ku Klux Klan. The federal government reported:

---

[81] Rawick, ed., The American Slave, Part 2, Vol. 4, 73 (Mattie Gilmore); Part 4, Vol. 5, 14 (Hannah Scott); Elizabeth Silverthorne, Plantation Life in Texas (College Station: Texas A&M University Press, 1986), 209; Tyler, The Slave Narratives of Texas, 125.

[82] Laura Ray, File 4J295, Cherokee County, Works Progress Administration Records, Center for American History, Barker History Collection, University of Texas, Austin.

[83] Rawick, ed., The American Slave, Part 4, Vol. 5, 75 (Emma Taylor); Emma Taylor, 4J295, Tyler, Texas, Works Progress Administration Records, Center for American History, Barker History Collection, University of Texas, Austin.

[84] Rawick, ed. The American Slave, Part 2, Vol. 4, 289 (Nancy King).

[85] Rawick, ed., The American Slave, Part 4, Vol. 5, 39 (Jordan Smith); File, "Slavery Life Under the Peculiar Institution," Harrison County Historical Museum, Marshall, Texas; Norman Yetman, ed., Slavery Life Under the Peculiar Institution (Lawrence: University of Kansas, 1970), 289.

Katie Darling

*Born in Slavery: Slave Narratives from the Federal Writers' Project,
1936-1938. Slave Narratives, Federal Writers Project, Manuscript
Division, Library of Congress, Washington, DC.*

"they shoot, cut, and maltreat them when they feel like it, and in some portions of this subdistrict a perfect reign of terror exists."[86] Hannah Jameson stated she remembered the Klan raging and beating folks. "That's the reason ma and my step-pa stayed with my old Master. He protect them."[87]

In some instances, according to historian Smallwood, "Freedpeople with kindly former owners voluntarily remained at their old jobs because their former owners had treated them fairly well." Lucy Lewis stayed with her former master a few months after emancipation. She explained why she changed her mind and decided to leave. Lucy initially "didn't want to be free because she was content working for missy, her former mistress. But, after a few months, she felt she had to be free, jus' like the others."[88]

Many freedwomen left their former slave owners because they wanted to make their own decisions. Specifically, they desired to take care of their own families without any restrictions. They enabled themselves to do this by relying upon a government agency, the Bureau of Refugees, Freedmen's and Abandoned Lands, better known as the Freedmen's Bureau.

In essence, this section shows that during slavery, freedpeople, with emphasis on women, endured slavery due to the family which gave them strength. Slave women used whatever means to be wives and mothers in spite of slavery. Slave women, as mothers, took care of their children and gave them advice on how to survive slavery. Furthermore, slave women often gave their children labor advice. They acted as wives even when their slave husbands resided on another plantation. They refused to give up hope that slavery would end, and at the same

---

[86] Gregory Barrett, SAC, to Charles Vernon, SAC, Tyler Texas, August 31, 1868; Vol. 162, p. 219, Letters Sent, BRFAL, RG 105, NA.

[87] Hannah Jameson, File 4H357, Marshall, Texas, Works Progress Administration Records, Center for American History, Barker History Collection, University of Texas, Austin.

[88] James Smallwood, "Black Texans During Reconstruction," East Texas Historical Journal 14 (Spring 1976): 10; Rawick, ed., The American Slave, Part 3, Vol. 5, 16 (Lucy Lewis).

time, they looked forward to having the right to their make their own choices. Thus, slave woman in East Texas endured slavery, and at the same time fashioned a slave family. After slavery, they dealt with their family demands by utilizing the services of the Freedmen's Bureau to assist them in making social and labor decisions that had been denied to them as slaves. The Freedmen's Bureau enabled freedwomen to assume responsibility for familial duties within and outside the household. Overall, the family served as the focal point for survival with the Bureau providing assistance.

Born in Slavery: Slave Narratives from the Federal Writers' Project, 1936-1938. Slave Narratives, Federal Writers Project, Manuscript Division, Library of Congress, Washington, DC.

CHAPTER 4

The Freedmen's Bureau & Freedwomen: Reconstruction In Texas With Emphasis On Judicial & Civil Issues, 1865-1872

Reconstruction in Texas marked a new beginning for newly freed Texas slaves with freedwomen at the forefront in meeting the challenges of emancipation. Freedwomen, along with freedmen, sought the assistance of the Bureau of Refugees, Freedmen, and Abandoned Lands, to help meet the demands of Reconstruction. The Reconstruction Era presented new challenges for freedpeople because now they had the opportunity to determine their own destiny at home, in the community, and in the labor force. Reconstruction in the former confederacy, including East Texas, began in 1865 after the Civil War when the federal government faced the task of rebuilding the nation.

To reconstruct the nation, President Abraham Lincoln and Congress had to decide how to rebuild the nation, and how to assist the freedpeople in adjusting to freedom. They debated on how to handle social, economic, and civil issues affecting the freedpeople. Radical

Republicans in Congress, led by Thaddeus Stevens and Benjamin Wade advised President Abraham Lincoln to draft a plan to accomplish these aims of reuniting the nation, rebuilding the south, and assisting the freedpeople. The president's plan to restore the Union would have granted amnesty to ex-Confederate officials. Radical Republicans in Congress opposed the plan because they believed that supporters of the former Confederacy should be punished for treason against the nation. They decided to draft their own plan which would have disqualified ex-Confederates from holding office, and addressed issues concerning the freedpeople.

Lincoln appeared unwilling to accept Congress's plan for Reconstruction, and before they could resolve their differences, an actor known as John Wilkes Booth, assassinated the president in April 1865. Vice President Andrew Johnson, a southern Democrat became President and assumed the responsibility with Congress for Reconstruction. Johnson ignored Congress, and attempted to implement his own plan. Nevertheless, the Repubicans became the victors, and carried forth their plan for Radical Reconstruction, to include the operation of the Freedmen's Bureau. It already had been established in March 1865 to assist former slaves and improverished whites in employment, health programs, legal aid in labor or wages contract disputes, and in the development of schools. General Oliver O. Howard became Commissioner of the Bureau the same year, and assumed responsibility for its operations. Congress had originally planned for the Bureau to last for one year, but extended it to meet the needs of indigent white southeners and freedpeople. It "renewed the Bureau in 1866 over President Andrew Johnson's veto and every year thereafter until 1870."[89]

The Bureau entered Texas in September 1865, and the first assistant commissioner for Texas, General Edgar M. Gregory, aggressively pursued a vigorous reconstruction program comprised of social and

---

[89] James M. Smallwood, "Black Texans During Recontruction: First Freedom," East Texas Historical Journal 14 (Spring 1976): 18.

economic reforms designed to assist the freedpeople in their transition from slavery to freedom. The Bureau's assistant commissioners in Texas, were admonished "to do all that they could to promote mutual good will among blacks and whites, by a spirit of fairness, great discretion, and the broadest possible charity." Howard warned in his earliest general letter of advice to assistant commissioners, "all the disturbing elements of the old system of industry and society are around you." Therefore, Howard alerted his subordinates to the enormous tasks of performing their duties amongst opposition from ex-Confederates.[90]

The Texas assistant commissioners worked hard to carry out the Bureau policies, and they faced many challenges during Reconstruction in Texas. During General Edgar M. Gregory's tenure, he worked to refine the labor system and to extend full citizenship rights to the freedpeople. However, he did promote education for the freedpeople. On May 14, 1866, Joseph Kiddoo replaced Gregory as assistant commissioner. Joseph Kiddoo focused his attention on education and justice, along with labor concerns of the freedpeople. Charles Griffin replaced Kiddoo on January 24, 1867. He increased Bureau manpower and area supervision. Reynolds, the last assistant commissioner in Texas, assumed his position in late 1867. He focused on political matters concerning the freedpeople, and he worked to provide freedpeople with more economic rights and continued to emphasize education.

According to historian Crouch, all the assistant commissioners in Texas tried to improve conditions for the freedpeople. To accomplish this purpose, they assigned tasks to agents to direct and supervise specific sections of the state divided into subdistricts to accomodate the size of the state. The subdistrict generally comprised from two to five counties with different racial compositions. The subassistant commissioner stationed in Tyler, the thirtieth subdistrict, had jurisdiction over Smith County and adjacent areas in East Texas, specifically the areas covered in this

---

[90] Smallwood, "Black Texans During Reconstruction," 18; General Edgar Gregory, Assistant Commissioner, to Oliver O. Howard, Commissioner, Galveston, Texas, March 3, 1866; MIC-821, n.p., Letters Sent, BRFAL, RG 105, NA.

study.[91] The activities of Bureau officials in the areas of civil justice and education will be examined to determine their effectiveness in working with freedpeople, with emphasis on women during the time. The Bureau courts supervised by Bureau agents assumed significant roles in Reconstruction East Texas. Bureau officials in Texas courts pretended to act as justices of the peace to protect the civil rights of freedpeople, including freedwomen. As justices of the peace they did not need legal training to carry out their duties. Therefore, despite the fact Bureau officials may not have had any legal training, they still served as "counsel, judge, and jury," to many African-Americans. Although this system posed shortcomings in protecting the rights of freedpeople, it appeared to be the only system they could rely on. Furthermore, Bureau officials monitored trials in cases in "which they did not have jurisdiction" to insure African-Americans would receive justice.[92] Specifically, Bureau agents had legal jurisdiction over African-Americans when state courts violated African-Americans' rights. Many times African-American women fought for their rights in Bureau supervised courts.

Through the use of Bureau courts, the federal government intervened in the justice system to protect the civil and property rights of freedwomen. In addition, the federal government intervened in civil dispute cases concerning East Texas African-American women. Many of these cases involved non-payment of debts. Females served as witnesses in civil cases concerning non-payment of monies due either for services or property. In addition, the Bureau arbitrated civil property complaints involving African-American women fighting for their property rights. Martha Ann Richardson sued Norwood and Curly because they "had seized her property without due authority." This case failed to be settled because both "parties failed to appear."[93]

---

[91]   Barry A. Crouch, The Freedmen's Bureau and Black Texans (Austin: University of Texas Press, 1992), 38-42.

[92]   Crouch, The Freedmen's Bureau, 51.

[93]   Martha Ann Richardson, freedwoman, vs. Norwood and Curly, Tyler, Texas, September 20, 1867; Vol. 164, p. 77, Register of Complaints, BRFAL, RG 105, NA.

This was a common occurrence because freedpeople were afraid of retaliation. Overall, misdemeanors cases such as theft appeared to be common in civil cases.

In addition to civil cases, East Texas African-American women became involved in criminal cases. A freedwoman, Jane Brewer had been accused of stealing from Emma Appleton, a gold ring, a bottle of cologne, a dressing comb, and some boiled soap. The Bureau dismissed this case due to lack of evidence. Another case involved two freedwomen accused of assault and battery upon each other. Violet Jones and Mary Pompey both worked illegally as prostitutes. The judge advised both of them to get a job when they reported to his court.[94]

Also, a proportion of civil cases involved sexual assault and rape against freedwomen. They had experienced many problems with white men attempting to maintain the sexual mores of the slavery period, which included rape and sexual exploitation.[95] Historian Bell hooks states that "most sexual assaults on black women occurred on the job . . . most white men often coerced black women into sexual liaisons by threatening to fire them unless they consented to sexual demands."[96] According to Gerda Lerner, "the rape of African-American women is employed as a weapon of terror directed against the entire African-American community." White men then appeared to use African-American women as sex objects.[97] Ann Doomis, a freedwoman, testified that she had witnessed John Crumb rape a freedwoman who worked for him. Crumb's lawyer persuaded the jury "not to take the testimony of a negro . . .". Due to fears of an uprising between whites and African-Americans, the judge acquitted Crumb. The Bureau opposed

---

[94] United States, vs. Violet Jones and Mary Pompey, Tyler, Texas, August 5, 1867, Vol. 164, p. 65-66; Emma Appleton, vs. Jane Brewer, Marshall, Texas, November 10, 1868, Vol. 136, p.62; Register of Complaints, BRFAL, RG 105, NA.

[95] Smallwood, Time of Hope, Time of Despair, 33.

[96] Bell hooks, Ain't I A Woman: Black Women and Feminism (Boston: South End Press, 1981), 56-57.

[97] Gerda Lerner, ed. Black Women in White America: A Documentary History (New York: Random House, Inc., 1972), 149.

this decision and requested Crumb to appear before the Bureau court. The records did not reveal whether Crumb reported.[98]

The Freedmen's Bureau records contain frequent complaints of rape or attempted rape of African-American women by both, white and black men. In Nacogdoches, Frank Morris, a freedman attempted to rape freedwoman, Sophia. He had to work two months for the county for committing this act.[99] Of course, the decision may have been different if Morris was a white man, because according to Mary Berry, based on southern states with cases involving white men and freedwomen, "judges often failed to prosecute white men accused of using force to seduce or rape African-American women."[100] However, the Texas courts prosecuted several white men for attempting to rape freedwomen. One such case involved freedwoman, Fanny Whetstone and two white men. Fanny Whetstone reported that Anthony Coon, "formerly a soldier belonging to Co. C. 15th Infantry," "entered her house and threw" her on the bed and wanted to have "criminal intercourse with" her, which she refused. Afterwards, another man with Coon whose name is unknown threw himself on top of Fanny while she was in the bed. In the process of the act, Coon struck her in the face with his fist, thus "causing the blood to flow all over" her dress. She managed to get away from both men, and reported the incident to the bureau. The bureau issued a warrant for the arrest of both men. Squire Hall tried the case and fined the defendant one dollar and court costs. Thus, the case was settled.[101]

---

[98]   Gregory Barrett, SAC, Tyler, Texas, to Charles Vernou, Austin, Texas, June 6, 1868; Vol. 162, pp. 165-66, Letters Sent, BRFAL, RG 105, NA.

[99]   Sophia, freedwoman, vs. Frank Morris, freedman, Nacogdoches, Texas, December 8, 1868; Vol. 140, pp. 16-17, BRFAL, RG 105, NA.

[100] Mary Berry, "Judging Morality: Sexual Behavior and Legal Consequences in the Late Nineteenth-Century South," The Journal of American History 78 (December 1991): 849; Gerda Lerner, ed., Black Women in White America: A Documentary History (New York: Random House Inc., 1972), 163-64.

[101] Fanny Whetstone, freedwoman, vs. Anthony Coon, Marshall, Texas, November 21, 1868; Vol. 136, p. 73, BRFAL, RG 105, NA.

The federal government investigated criminal cases involving assaults, murder, and theft committed by and against African-American women because the local authorities tended to disregard abusive treatment of African-American women. Oftentimes, local judicial officials refused to hear any charges brought by an African-American against a white person. In many instances when the Bureau pursued charges against whites by African-Americans, it proved ineffective because Texas had a law which stated "that persons of color shall not testify, except when the prosecution is against a person who is a person of color; or where the offence is committed against the person or property of a person of color."[102] Therefore, African-American women often fought a losing battle against white men and women who violated them due to restrictions placed upon them. Despite such obstacles, freedwomen still presented cases against whites to the Freedmen's Bureau which served as their judge and jury.

To insure that freedpeople, including freedwomen, would appear for their cases against whites, the bureau considered providing armed protection for the freedpeople. Barrett acknowledged that Tyler lacked troops, and stated, "the freedpeople are not as secure as when the troops were here." He concluded that the "civil authorities would not do" the freedpeople justice. [103]

In many instances, freedpeople depended upon the Bureau to provide protection. However, in spite of Bureau assistance, assaults and murders against freedpeople continued with alarming frequency. Two whites killed an African-American female domestic servant named Lucy Grimes in Harrison County because she refused to punish her child for stealing money. On February 20, 1866, Lieutenant Colonel

---

[102] Report of Bvt. Major General J.B. Kiddoo, for the year ending December 31, 1866, BRFAL, RG 105, NA.

[103] Henry Sweeney, SAC, to Joseph Reynolds, Assistant Commissioner (AC), Jefferson, Texas, December 14, 1868; Vol. 116, n. p., Letters Sent; Gregory Barrett, SAC, Tyler, Texas, to Charles A. Vernou, Acting Assistant Adjutant General (AAAG), Austin, Texas, June 1, 1868; Vol. 162, p. 157, Letters Sent, BRFAL, RG 105, NA.

H. S. Hall testified before Congress that the murder of Lucy Grimes in Marshall had gone unpunished. She had been beaten to death by two "discharged rebel soldiers" named Anderson and Simpson, who went free because no witnesses would testify against them except freedpeople. Her offense, Hall said, had been "to refuse to whip her child who had been accused of stealing."[104]

Furthermore, Hall informed Congress that military forces should remain in Marshall due to rampant violence against freedpeople. In his opinion, freedpeople "would be liable to worse treatment than ever before, to assaults in many cases, and even to murder," if the troops left the area.[105] In Tyler, James Thornton murdered a freedwoman named Julia Richardson for an unknown reason. Thornton was arrested and placed in the Tyler jail, and later he was turned over to the sheriff of Henderson County to allow the civil authorities to prosecute the case.[106] James Landtrift hanged Ellen Mc Carthy. A warrant was issued for his arrest, and he was "placed in the hands of the sheriff."[107]

Many freedpeople survived assaults upon them by local whites. They would express dissatisfaction with such assaults. In some instances, husbands would come to their wife's defense. Orange Bray protested the whipping his wife had received from his former master. As a result, the former master attempted to whip him for insolence, but Orange used an ax to defend himself against any abuse. Despite Orange's actions, the former master shot Bray and a "Lamar county jury sentenced Bray to the penitentiary while his former owner went free."[108] This demonstrates that African-American men did not always

---

[104] United States House of Representatives, House Reports, 39th Congress, 1st Session, 1866, Report No. 30, 47 (first quotation), 46.

[105] Ibid., Report No. 46 (second quotation), 50.

[106] United States vs. James Thornton, Tyler, Texas, June 10, 1868; Vol. 163, pp. 20-21, Register of Complaints, BRFAL, RG 105, NA.

[107] United States vs. James Landtrift, Tyler, Texas, June 11, 1868; Vol. 163, pp. 18-19, Register of Complaints, BRFAL, RG 105, NA.

[108] Alwyn Barr, Black Texans: A History of Negroes in Texas, 1528-1971 (Austin: Jenkins Publishing Co., 1973), 42-43.

tolerate the worse abuses committed against them or their wives, without defending themselves.[109]

Joe Raines complained to the Bureau that Jas Morrefield had assaulted his wife. The resolution of the case was not revealed. However, it does show that African-American women could occasionally depend on African-American men to protect them.[110]

In spite of African-American efforts to defend themselves, the Bureau reported that whites continued to abuse freedwomen, as well as freedmen, and threatened the women if they testified against them. Many times they went to the Bureau for assistance regarding such threats. The Bureau intervened in some cases involving assaults upon African-American women who testified against their assailants. It fined Robert McKinley $40 for assaulting Susan Manning. McKinley had "choked her violently while lying sick in bed." In another case, John Forrester had assaulted Margaret Jones. The court fined Forrester $25.[111] In Marshall, McAkin, a white man, paid a $50 fine for assaulting Vira Comer, a freedwoman. Also in Marshall, Texas, Hattie Burke, a freedwoman was stabbed in the abdomen. She had been told by the doctor that she would die within 24 hours so she made a statement that the prisoner brought before her, William Tincher, witnessed another soldier stab her. Tincher refused to help her, and he closed the door to prevent her screams from being heard. She identified Acera Brown as the one who had stabbed her. The bureau ordered Tincher and Brown to be arrested and placed in the Post Guard house.[112] The cases show

[109] Smallwood, Time of Hope, Time of Despair, 127.

[110] Joe Raines, freedman, vs. Jas Morrefield, Tyler, Texas, September 21, 1868; Vol. 163, p. 32, Register of Complaints, BRFAL, RG 105, NA.

[111] Susan Manning, freedwoman, vs. Robert McKinley, Smith County, Texas, July 5, 1867, Vol. 164, p. 52; Margaret Jones, freedwoman, vs. John Forrester, Tyler, Texas, July 16, 1867, Vol. 164, p. 57, Register of Complaints, BRFAL, RG 105, NA.

[112] The United States in Account with Andrew Mallory, to Edward Henshaw, SAC, Marshall, Texas, July 1, 1867, Vol. 136, p. 18; Hattie Burke, freedwoman, vs. William Tincher, Marshall, Texas, November 20, 1868, Vol. 136, p. 70-71, Register of Complaints, BRFAL, RG 105, NA.

that freedwomen made attempts to report abuses committed against them to the Bureau.

Freedwomen not only needed protection from individuals, but they also required protection from white supremacist groups. It did not take much effort to convince the Bureau that freedpeople needed some protection due to the actions of white supremacist groups. In Texas, the Klu Klux Klan, a white supremacist organization, known as the Knights of the Rising Sun, used any and every kind of intimidation and violence against the freedpeople and their supporters. According to Bureau agent Sweeney, "whipping the freedmen, robbing them of their arms, driving them off plantations, and murdering whole families are of daily, and nightly occurrence, all done by disguised parties whom no one can testify to . . . the civil authorities never budge an inch to try and discover these midnight marauders and apparently a perfect apathy exists throughout the whole community regarding the general state of society . . . nothing but martial law can save this section . . ."[113] In Marshall, Rand believed freedpeople would have no justice if troops were removed from the area.[114]

In addition to the Bureau, African-American women often had to look to former paternalistic owners for protection and assistance. Hannah Jameson remembered "the Klan raging and beatin folks . . . that's the reason ma and my stepp-pa stayed with my old Master.' He protect them."[115]

In another incident, a bandit named Dixon, forced an old African-American woman named Aunt Daphne to dance until "she was exhausted and then she was told to get on her knees beside a log and to pray." "While she was praying he stabbed her in the back and went

[113] Henry Sweeney, SAC, to Charles Roberts, SAC, Jefferson, Texas, October 31, 1868; Vol. 116, n. p., Letters Sent, BRFAL, RG 105, NA.
[114] Charles Rand, SAC, to Henry Ellis, AAC, Marshall, Texas, January 10, 1867; Vol. 134, p. 5, Letters Sent, BRFAL, RG 105, NA.
[115] Hannah Jameson, file 4H357, Marshall, Texas, Works Progress Administration Records, Center for American History, Barker History Collection, University of Texas, Austin.

on his way." Dixon was later killed by a company of African-American soldiers who had been informed of his whereabouts by Merritt Trammell, a former slave preacher, and the leader of African-Americans in Limestone county area.[116]

Violence against freedpeople attracted the attention of state government officials who reluctantly decided to allow the Bureau to interfere in state problems concerning abuses against freedpeople. Andrew Hamilton, provisional Governor of Texas appointed by President Andrew Johnson, reported, "there is scarcely a day, that I am not informed of a homicide committed upon a Freedman. I have no power either to prevent these abuses, or punish the offenders. It must be obvious to you, General, as it is to me, that we cannot depend upon the Civil Authority in our State, for sometime yet, to deal out justice to evil doers. It is true, I have appointed civil officers for the several Counties; but in very many of them, process could not be executed, on any one of a gang of outlaws, who openly defy the civil authority, and in many of the Counties, I am satisfied, that judges, jurors, and witnesses, would all be in danger unless protected by the Military power of the General government."[117]

Historian William S. McFeeley argues that Bureau commissioner Oliver O. Howard charged his subordinate assistant commissioners with responsibility for collecting detailed evidence of outrages perpetrated by whites against freedpeople, thereby hoping to accumulate evidence that the Bureau was in fact still needed to shape Reconstruction.[118] Howard's actions to justify the Bureau's role in Texas during Reconstruction—gathering reports of outrages and then prosecuting the offenders—became one of the Bureau's principal roles in protecting the rights of the freedpeople. The Bureau's evidence further revealed

---

[116] Doris Pemberton, Juneteenth at Comanche Crossing (Austin: Eakin Publishing, 1983), 60.

[117] Andrew Hamilton to Horatio Wright, September 27, 1865, Hamilton Papers, Texas State Library, Austin, Texas.

[118] William S. McFeely, Yankee Stepfather: General O. O. Howard and the Freedmen (New Haven: Yale University Press, 1978), 200-201.

that in addition to abuses from whites, freedwomen encountered abuses from freedmen. Many Bureau reports contained complaints made by African-American women regarding their treatment from African-American men. Leanna Greer, a freedwoman reported Sam McGregor, a freedman, for assaulting her. The agent summoned McGregor who failed to appear for the case.[119] John Douglass assaulted Bell Scott, so he had to pay a fine.[120] Hilda Henson reported that Edmund Huff jumped on her and beat her, and therefore she wanted him to be arrested. The Bureau decided that Hilda had provoked Edmund to hit her and that he had only hit her with his open hand after she had grossly and repeatedly insulted him. The Bureau also said that Hilda was quarrelsome, and that she had an unsocial disposition, and therefore warned both of them that they would be arrested if their behavior continued.[121]

Other conflicts persisted between African-American men and African-American women. Agnes Ewell, a freedwoman in Marshall, complained that she had brought six acres of land from Hayden Ware, a freedman, and he had agreed to accept a mule as payment. Agnes paid for the land as agreed, but Ware refused to give her the deed for the land. Ware had promised to deed six acres to her as soon as he had the deed from Mr. Duncan who was the present owner, or either he would pay her for the mule. Agnes had made improvements on the property and the land, so she wanted the property. The Bureau resolved the case upon Agnes's consent to wait until Mr. Duncan gave the deed to Ware who in return would give it to her.[122] Celia Washington complained

---

[119] Leanna Greer, freedwoman, vs. Sam McGregor, freedman, Tyler, Texas, March 30, 1868; Vol. 163, pp. 6-7, Register of Complaints, BRFAL, RG 105, NA.

[120] Bell Scott, freedwoman, vs. John Douglass, freedman, Tyler, Texas, May 2, 1868; Vol. 163, pp. 12-13, Register of Complaints, BRFAL, RG 105, NA.

[121] Hilda Henson, freedwoman, vs. Edmund Huff, freedman, Marshall, Texas, November 7, 1868; Vol. 136, p. 58, Register of Complaints, BRFAL, RG 105, NA.

[122] Agnes Ewell, freedwoman, vs. Hayden Ware, freedman, Marshall, Texas, November 5, 1868; Vol. 136, p. 54, BRFAL, RG 105, NA.

that Jack Williams refused to pay $11 he had borrowed from her. As a result of her complaint, the Bureau issued a warrant for Williams arrest. Williams had to pay Celia the amount he owed and $1.50 for the Sheriff's services used in arresting him.[123] Another freedman, Charles Holt refused to pay Eliza Williams, a freedwoman, for a pair of shoes he had received from her. When Eliza asked him to pay her for the shoes, he assaulted her and refused to pay her. She filed a complaint against Holt with the Bureau. Holt failed to report to the Bureau as requested, therefore the case was dismissed until a later date. The records failed to show whether the Bureau resolved this case.[124]

Civil cases involving freedwomen increased during Reconstruction in East Texas. Freedwomen reported civil complaints because they believed that the Bureau would help them. The Bureau handled many civil cases involving African-Americans because the local legal authorities failed to resolve complaints dealing with African-Americans civil or human rights. As a matter of fact, many times local authorities committed acts against the African-Americans and protected whites who abused African-Americans. In Tyler this had happened to Malinda Lewis who reported that Judge Stewart had committed assault and battery upon her when she presented her case against her white employer. Likewise in another case, Judge Stewart had refused to give up a certain amount of clothing promised to Harriett Sharp.[125]

Local authorities continued to suppress the civil rights of the freedpeople because ex-Confederates who had gained judicial power objected to any enforcement of the laws by the Bureau to protect the

---

[123] Celia Washington, freedwoman, vs. Jack Williams, freedman, Tyler, Texas, April 16, 1868; Vol. 164, pp. 10-11, Register of Complaints, BRFAL, RG 105, NA.

[124] Eliza Williams, freedwoman, vs. Charles Holt, freedman, Tyler, Texas, July 16, 1867; Vol. 164, p. 57, Register of Complaints, BRFAL, RG 105, NA.

[125] Malinda Lewis, freedwoman, vs. Judge Stewart, Tyler, Texas, April 13, 1867, Vol. 164, p. 18; Harriet Sharp, freedwoman, vs. Judge Sharp, Tyler, Texas, April 13, 1867, Vol. 164, p. 18, Register of Complaints, BRFAL, RG 105, NA.

freedpeople. In January of 1868 a new Commissioner, General Winfield Scott Hancock, a Union General, undermined the limited ability of the Bureau to protect the rights and regulate labor for the freepeople. He agreed with President Johnson's policy of rapid restoration which neglected the rights of the freedpeople, although he knew a conflict existed between federal officials and state authorities who supported white supremacy. Hancock failed to address this problem. Instead, he occupied himself with the Bureau's administrative affairs; and, he ordered his subordinates to rely on civil authorities to enforce the law instead of the Bureau. Afterwards, the freedwomen and freedmen lost judicial and civil rights they had hoped to keep.[126]

---

[126]   Smallwood, Time of Hope, Time of Despair, 57; Charles Rand, SAC, to Henry Ellis, Marshall, Texas, January 10, 1868, Vol. 134, n. p., Letters Sent; Thomas Smith, SAC, to Charles Vernon, SAC, Marshall, Texas, July 31, 1868, Vol. 134, n. p., Letters Sent, BRFAL, RG 105, NA.

CHAPTER 5

Texas Freedwomen And Education in
The African-American Community, 1865-1875

The American Missionary Association, the Freedmen's Bureau and freedpeople acquired support from religious associations, as well as African-American churches, to finance schools and provide teachers. The aid societies and African-American churches provided the majority of teachers for African-American schools. For example, in September of 1865, teachers recruited by the African Methodists opened Houston's first African-American school, an achievement hampered only by the complaints of local whites who said that the teachers taught "young blacks to love northern soldiers." Other societies, the Freedmen's Aid Society and the Methodist Episcopal Missionary Society, also became prominent suppliers of teachers and helped establish schools.[127]

Northern white members of the Methodist Episcopal Church organized the Freedmen's Aid Society, "a spin-off of the Freedmen's

---

[127] Galveston Daily News, October 1, November 12, 1865; Henry Lee Swint, The Northern Teacher in the South, 1862-1870 (New York: Octagon Books, 1967), 175; Walter F. Cotton, History of Negroes of Limestone County from 1860 to 1939 (Mexia: J.A. Chatman and S. M. Merriwether, 1939), 17; James Hutchinson, Agent, to James Kirkman, SAC, Columbia, Texas, April 30, 1867, Letters Sent, Vol. 78, n.p., BRFAL, RG 105, NA.

Bureau staffed by Quakers." It encouraged young African-American female students to become teachers, and favored hiring them at the schools. It stated, "there are in all our schools young women who would make good missionaries for their sex," and the "proper candidates for this work could be named by the principals of the schools."[128] The Society became active in educating African-Americans in Limestone county, and encouraged African-American female students to become teachers. Another society, the Congregationalist American Missionary Society also provided teachers and aid to African-American schools.[129]

In East Texas, the local presbytery of the Presbyterian Church assisted in the education of freedpeople beginning in 1867. A report of the Education Committee of the Eastern Texas Presbytery reported, "in some places our ministers have been preaching to the colored people with some degree of encouragement." Two of the ministers had large congregations of African-Americans. One minister had "a flourishing Sabbath School under his supervision."[130]

Benevolent groups also provided assistance to African-American schools whenever possible. They provided bibles and hymn books to freedpeople. Because the associations could not meet all demands, teachers such as Sarah Barnes of Galveston constantly requested more materials only to be turned down. Serious teaching problems resulted, with teachers being handicapped by school supply shortages. However, the assistance received from the groups enabled the school to remain open.[131]

---

[128]   Methodist Episcopal Church, Eleventh Annual Report of the Freedmen's Aid Society (Cincinnati: Western Methodist Book Concern Print, 1879), 18.

[129]   Doris H. Pemberton, Juneteenth at Comanche Crossing (Austin: Eaking Publishing, 1983), 56; Alwyn Barr, Black Texans: A History of Negroes in Texas, 1528-1971, 62.

[130]   Minutes of the Presbytery of Eastern Texas, Presbyterian Church in the United States, 1870, vol. III, p. 27, Austin, Texas.

[131]   Barnes to Secretary, American Bible Society, March 23, 1868, Barnes to Strieby, May 5, 1868, Elijah Gerrow to Smith, December 30, 1868, Gonzales to Secretary of the American Missionary Association, February 4, 1870, Austin, Texas collection, AMA Archives, microfilm at the University of Maryland at College Park, Maryland.

A school in Marshall had a night session for adults and "those deprived of the privilege of attending during the theday."[132] The freedpeople paid tuition and books, and the teacher's pay was supplemented by a small monthly sum, "sufficient to defray the tuition of those who are too poor to pay the stipulated fee."[133]

The Bureau visited African-American schools in the Houston area to "persuade the freedpeople to send their children to school," to take advantage of the free school in the area.[134] Children attended such schools due to the efforts of freedwomen and freedmen who provided provisions such as books and school supplies for the maintenance and education of children and orphans. Schoolteacher, Miss Campbell, took some orphans into her school without any fee.[135]

The editor of the Harrison Flag opposed northern control of freedmen schools with northern teachers, but acknowledged that African-Americans needed an education in order to become "good citizens."[136] Influenced by this editorial, some whites in Harrison County later established an African-American school on the Shreveport-Marshall railroad at Wascum station, a settlement of African-American workers and their families, which included 300 to 400 children." This school marked a unique incident because educational aid given to African-Americans from white Texans proved to be the exception rather than the rule, because most whites remained hostile or indifferent to African-American schools. Occassionally, white churches led the opposition to African-American education. Their consensus was that

---

132 Reort of Brevet Major General J. B. Kiddoo, Assistant Commissioner for Texas, for the year ending December 31, 1866, p. 4, RG 105, NA, Washington, D.C.

133 Report of the Assistant Commissioner for Texas, 1866, for the year ending October 31, 1866, p.8, Brevet Major General J. B. Kiddoo, Assistant Commissioner for Texas, RG 105, NA, Washington, D.C.

134 Records of the Assistant Commissioner for the State of Texas, Sub-assistant Commissioner Report, C.A. Dempsey, October 15, 1866, p. 266, RG 105, NA, Washington, D.C.

135 Mrs. Fannie Campbell to George Whipple, AMA, November 24, 1866, Austin, Texas.

136 Harrison Flag (Marshall), May 2, 1867.

if African-Americans received an education, "they would become too independent, too politically and socially aware, and then might upset the southern way of life."[137] Furthermore, many whites in Texas feared education for African-Americans due to the Memphis riot of 1866. This riot led to "opposition . . . in many other sections of the South in 1866." African-American churches and schools were burned, thus forcing many whites to abandon their work with freedpeople.[138] Whites in Clarksville showed no efforts to promote education. They believed no good would result from an education system for African-Americans. Therefore, the school open for African-Americans closed its doors.[139]

African-American newspapers encouraged schools for African-Americans to remain open and promote education. To emphasize the importance of education, the Freedman's Press informed freedpeople newspapers "will be sent free to every clergyman of the colored people in the State, and to all of colored schools. Send us your name."[140] This marked an increased effort to recruit African-American teachers and to encourage African-Americans to acquire an education. In Tyler two schools for freedpeople had been established due to financial support from the Bureau and teachers supplied by the northern missionary societies. The schools employed a northern white female teacher, namely Mary Stripling and Henry Black, an African-American. In June 1868, Mary Stripling had sixty-two pupils in her day school, and seventy-five pupils in the Sunday school. By August 31, 1868 she had only thirty-five pupils in her day school, and fifty pupils in the Sunday school. Mr. Black had only twenty-five pupils in his day school, and zero enrollment in the Sunday school. Attendance had probably decreased in both schools due to the crop season which depended upon

---

[137] Smallwood, Time of Hope, Time of Despair, 76-77.
[138] American Missionary, X, 6 (June, 1866), 134-135; X, 10 (October, 1866), 223-224; Barry A. Crouch, "Hidden Sources of Black History: The Texas Freedmen's Bureau Records As A Case Study," Southwestern Historical Quarterly 83 (January 1980), 223.
[139] George Sharkley, SAC, to Roberts, Agent, Miscellaneous Reports, October 31, 1868, Clarksville, Box 39, RG 105, NA, Vol. 130.
[140] Freedman's Press (Austin), July 18, 1868, p. 2.

the labor of the students in the fields.[141] Although many freedpeople had to miss school to work in the fields, Tyler's school progress was fair. The school was expected to do better after the crop season because money was scarce, and the freedpeople needed money from the crops to pay the tuition.[142]

African-American schools led by missionary societies had also flourished with the hiring of female teachers. As historian Brooks indicated, "their stated goal was to develop a cadre of black women leaders capable of providing basic education to many others."[143] In 1866, Fannie Campbell, operated a day school of eighty-seven students. She also operated an evening school of forty night students, and a very large Sabbath school of 200 students until the Methodists opened a Sabbath school in the basement of the church. The more her school succeeded, the more white church members complained. Not only did the school become too independent but Campbell conducted her Sunday classes while whites conducted theirs during the same time at the church. They complained to have Campbell's school taught at a different time. The children would not come to their school while "their colored school met at the same hour in the basement." She stood firm and refused to change the school schedule. Enrollment and attendance dropped when the schedule did change. As a result, her school attendance dropped from 200 to twenty. Finally, the Bureau made Campbell discontinue her classes.[144] Although Campbell had to close her school, she had

---

[141] Gregory Barrett to Charles Vernon, Letters Sent, June 30, 1868, August 31, 1868, Tyler, Texas, Vol. 162, RG 105, NA, Washington, D.C.

[142] Gregory Barrett to Charles Vernon, Letters Sent, June 30, 1868, Vol. 162, RG 105, NA, Washington, D.C.

[143] Anne Firor Scott, "Most Invisible of All: Black Women's Voluntary Associations," Journal of Southern History 56 (February 1990), 8.

[144] James W. Smallwood, "Black Education in Reconstruction Texas: Freedmen's Bureau and Benevolent Societies," East Texas Historical Journal 19 (January 1981), 26; Fannie Campbell to Whipple, November 24, 1866, American Missionary Association Archives with references to Schools and Mission Stations (hereinafter referred to as the AMA), Fisk University, Nashville, Tenn.: microfilm at the University of Maryland at College Park, College Park, Maryland ; BRFAL, Records of the Assistant

established a well planned curriculum for her students prior to her departure. She used first and second grade readers' textbooks in her classes. Students learned the alphabets, multiplication, "the capitals of the states and where situated," and "wrote letters and sung."[145]

Texas African-American women took it upon themselves to become more involved in education to educate and uplift the African-American race. African-American female networks provided tutorial services to assist African-American women in leading education reform. African-American and white female educators carried out education programs for freedpeople. Freedwoman, Annie Smith was among the educators in Van Zandt county. She taught classes in the local community and advised women to send their children to school.[146] In January 1868, in Paris, Texas, a freedwoman named Elizabeth Granger, assisted her husband, Charles in establishing a school. As a teacher, she enrolled sixty students, with forty-five attending regularly.[147]

A few African-American teachers had successful husbands and still continued to work as educators. Mrs. Jessie Warren of Smith county was married to one of Smith county's leading African-American citizens, a middle-class businessman. Although she did not have to work because her husband had a prosperous business, she still elected to work as an educator, becoming one of Tyler's leading educators.[148] Although Mrs.

Commissioner for the State of Texas, Sub-assistant Commissioner, Byron Porter to G. W. S. Brown, and W. S. Hotchkiss, Letters Sent, October 7, 1866, Austin, Texas, Vol. 48, RG 105, NA, Washington, D.C.

[145] Fannie Campbell to George Whipple, November 24, 1866, Austin, Texas, American Missionary Association Archives with references to Schools and Mission Stations, Fisk University, Nashville, Tenn.; microfilm at the University of Maryland at College Park.

[146] W. A. Redwine, Brief History of the Negro in Five Counties. Tyler, Texas: n.p., 1901; reprint, Chronicles of Smith County, Texas 11 (Fall 1972), 77.

[147] DeWitt Brown, SAC, to Edwin Wheelock, Superintendent of Schools, Paris, Texas, January 31, 1868; Vol. 20, n. p., Monthly Report, BRFAL, RG 105, NA.

[148] Redwine, Brief History of the Negro in Five Counties, 54. Mr. and Mrs. Jesse Warren, Tyler, Texas. Source: W. A. Redwine, Brief History of the Negro in Five Counties, Tyler, Texas: n.p., 1901; reprint, Chronicles of Smith County, Texas 11 (Fall 1972), 53.

Mitchell's husband had a prominent business in the local community, she continued to teach at the local school in Tyler. She was recognized as "one of the best experienced county teachers."[149]

Through the efforts of African-American women like Jessie Warren and Mrs. Mitchell, freedpeople demonstrated determination to exercise their right to have an education, and in some instances they taught themselves how to read and write. They also had an important role in the education process in the African-American community by especially providing guidance and educational support to their

children. Mothers encouraged disciplining their children to insure they would pay attention in class to get an education. One teacher in Hempstead county reported to Reverend Shepherd of the Freedmen's Aid Society of the Methodist Episcopal Church that she had the mothers' permission to discipline their children.[150] Examples of African-American parents' desire to have their children educated appeared repeatedly in the teachers reports submitted to the Bureau. One report indicated African-Americans "were anxious to have their children educated and were sadly in need of some kind man to direct their efforts, but they were not able to pay for such services." Fortunately, for some African-Americans, some people donated building lots. A man in Sandy Point named Mr. Terry built a school; planters in the neighborhood of Chance's Prairie gave a church to be used as a school. Columbus citizens pledged a church and a school, "but did not render the assistance on account of a dispute between two missionaries, one white and the other black, who came here to preach the gospel."[151]

African-American women not depending on churches to provide them with schools took it upon themselves to educate their children

---

[149] Ibid., 36

[150] William R. Davis, The Development and Present Status of Negro Education in East Texas (New York: Columbia University, 1934; reprint, New York: AMS Press, 1972), 31.

[151] James T. Kirkman, SAC, to Joseph Reynolds, AC, Columbus, Texas, Monthly Report, August 1, 1867, Vol. 78, pp.59-60, RG 105, NA, Washington, D.C.

at home. Mariah Earthman educated her children at home because her church did not provide schooling. Due to her perseverance, her daughter became a teacher, and was ranked "among the best teachers in Smith county."[152] In Tyler, Mrs. Polly Phillips educated her children.

Thus, the state focused its attention focused its attention on schools for white Texans while ignoring education for African-Americans. African-Americans felt discriminated against in education, because they felt deprived of a formal education, and yet they had to pay taxes to help support white schools in Texas. They believed they should have gained some educational benefits from their tax dollars. To enable them to acquire an education, they put emphasis on integration as a means to gain an education equal to whites. Therefore, freedpeople often gathered at conventions to declare their support of school integration. In 1873, they demanded at an African-American convention that they be guaranteed their rights. At the convention, they accused the "whites of steadfast opposition to their political, educational, and social progress, with a blind spirit of malignant opposition not calculated to inspire us with either confidence or affection." This convention demanded the passage of the civil rights bill and promised to agitate the question until African-Americans were guaranteed their rights. Furthermore, they stated, "we would far prefer to have received these rights as a voluntary offering from our white fellow-citizens." Unfortunately, Southern white men were determined to leave the colored people nothing to be grateful for, "as every right . . . has been forced from their grasp, in the face of stern opposition and openly expressed hatred." But the convention did not despair. It once again appealed for mutual cooperation "for the advancement of the interests of our state and the welfare of its citizens."[153] Texas white citizens ignored their requests, and continued to prevent African-Americans from attending school with whites. Therefore, African-American women and men realized they needed

---

[152] W. A. Redwine, Brief History of the Negro in Five Counties, 33.
[153] "Colored Men's Convention, July 3-4, 1873," in Eby, ed., Education in Texas, 581-84.

to assume full responsibility for education in the African-American community.

Shortly after Texans regained control of their governmental affairs, they instituted the community system of education for the state, a system which left the organization of schools optional with each local community. Texas adopted the community school system in 1876 as a "simple and inexpensive method for distributing the available state funds among the counties." As a result of this system, the school system had to be reorganized each year, and taxes could no longer be imposed.[154]

Overall, it appears that African-American women assumed very active roles in securing education for the African-American community. They taught school and participated in fundraisers for the schools. Women teachers must have performed very well because they had more students than the men. Also, more women than men taught school, in addition, statistics show that African-American women attended school at a higher rate than African-American men, and this was because African-American men had to work outside the household more often than women. In general, African-American women proved to be important in the education system for freedpeople throughout counties in Texas.

---

[154] William R. Davis, The Development and Present Status of Negro Education in East Texas, 41, 135.

CHAPTER 6

The Freedmen's Bureau & Freedwomen's Educational
Activities In East Texas, 1865-1872

During Reconstruction in East Texas, a drive for education for freedpeople gained momentum. Freedwomen and men themselves, the Freedmen's Bureau, and benevolent societies such as the American Missionary Association established schools. In September of 1865, under the direction of Texas superintendent of Education E. M. Wheelock, a Unitarian minister from New England, the Freedmen's Bureau established its first African-American school in Texas at Galveston with an enrollment of eighty students.[155]

The Freedmen's Bureau concentrated on establishing schools in the larger towns before focusing on the countryside. In this endeavor, E. M. Gregory, the Assistant Commissioner for Texas, assisted Wheelock. Gregory, labeled the "father of black education in Texas" by some contemporary scholars, encouraged missionaries to come to the state and, whenever possible, provided military protection to threatened schools.[156]

---

[155] John Thomas Hill, Jr., "The Negro in Texas During Reconstruction" (M. A., Texas Christian University, 1965), 78, 80.

[156] U.S. Senate, Senate Executive Documents, 39th Congress, 2nd session, 1867, no. 6, pp. 148-50, Washington, D. C.; C. S. Tambling to George Whipple, December 1, 1865, J.R.S. Van Vlect to Samuel Hunt, January

By January 1866, the Bureau had established ten day and six night schools in Texas with twenty teachers and 1,041 students, including many adults. By July 1866, the schools numbered ninety with forty-three teachers, and 4,590 students.[157] Most Bureau and teachers maintained night and Sabbath schools. The night schools offered education to adults and older children who worked during the day. The standards for the night schools were similar to day schools. The Sabbath schools enrolled both adults and children, and offered "biblical instruction" and "moral lessons."[158] According to historian Joe M. Richardson, "the teachers were to educate their pupils "into Christ," to rid them of their superstitious notions, and to teach morality."[159]

Many African-American students not enrolled in regular classes attended Sunday schools, and many teachers regarded their Sabbath classes as an extension of regular school where freedpeople who needed help could be taught the rudiments of reading and writing. The teachers held Sabbath classes in the basements of Baptist and Methodist churches (Figure 4.1). In 1866, the Texas state convention held in Austin, Texas, supported schools for African-Americans, separately

---

29, 1866, Texas correspondence, American Missionary Association, Amistad Research Center, Archives with references to Schools and Mission Stations, microfilm copies at the University of Maryland at College Park, Maryland, hereafter abbreviated AMA Archives; James W. Smallwood, "Black Education in Reconstruction Texas: The Contributions of the Freedmen's Bureau and Benevolent Societies," East Texas Historical Journal 19 (January 1981), 18.

[157] Alwyn Barr, Black Texans: A History of Negroes in Texas, 1528-1971 (Austin: Jenkins Publishing Co., 1973), 60-61; J. W. Alford, Report on Schools and Finances of Freedmen for July, 1866 (Washington, D.C.: 1866), 16.

[158] James W. Smallwood, "Education in Reconstruction Texas," 19; J. W. Alford, Third Semi-Annual Report on Schools for Freedmen (Washington, D.C., 1867), 28;

[159] Joe M. Richardson, Christian Reconstruction: The American Missionary Association and Southern Blacks, 1861-1890 (London; Athens: University of Georgia Press, 1986), 145. This is a pivotal study on American Missionary Association's activities in the South during and after Reconstruction.

of course. In spite of the convention's actions, many whites in Texas opposed the education of African-Americans, on the other hand, some whites believed that freedpeople should be assisted in developing a school system separate from whites, "to be sure, but a system decidedly evolutionary and ultimately destructive of caste."[160]

In the same year the Texas state convention declared: "In every neighborhood, on every plantation, and at all suitable places, let the negro, with the aid of the Southern people, build up schools. The negroes will contribute from their own labor and small resources. But white people must also help. In every way let the negro see that the Southern whites are his best friends. We must rise above the prejudices and avarices growing out of our past relations to the negro and recent political events, and be just and magnanimous."[161] The superintendent of education in Texas similarly expressed support to educate African-Americans. He went further and advocated educating freedpeople at any expense, "whether of money or of prejudice . . . to educate Negroes at public expense."[162]

Despite support from state officials to use public funds to educate freedpeople, the Texas constitution of 1866 specified public school funds be used exclusively for white students.[163] This action raised negative responses from African-Americans and some whites. Consequently, black education became an important issue in the African-American community. Later, the state also authorized the legislature to levy taxes for public education and to tax freedpeople for educational purposes.

---

[160] Texas State Teachers Association, Proceedings of the Texas Teachers' State Convention . . . 1866 (Louisville: John P. Morton and Co., 1866), 7-8.

[161] Texas State Teachers Association, Proceedings of the Texas Teachers' State Convention . . . 1866 (Louisville: John P. Morton and Co., 1866), 7-9; Frederick Eby, The Development of Education in Texas (New York: Macmillan Co., 1925), 106-107.

[162] Superintendent of Public Instruction E. M. Wheelock to Governor E. M. Pease, May 30, 1868, in Frederick Eby, ed., The Development of Education in Texas, 481.

[163] William R. Davis, The Development and Present Status of Negro Education in East Texas (New York: Columbia University, 1934; reprint, New York: AMS Press, 1972), 134-35.

Although the constitution stated "it should be a duty of the legislature to encourage schools among Negroes, nothing of the sort was done by the government which followed."[164]

In 1866 by Congressional legislative action, education was proposed for African-Americans throughout the South, including Texas, with the Freedmen's Bureau having primary responsibility.[165] The freedpeople encouraged the Bureau to carry out education activities. Agents recognized their desire for learning. In some areas, tuition was charged. Although a small amount, it really was a heavy tax on the freedpeople whose "average" wage did not exceed eight to fifteen dollars a month.[166]

Hence, the Bureau provided the most educational facilities and programs for freedpeople, of whom a large percentage were illiterate. Wheelock had established Bureau schools on a New England pattern. Classes began at 9:00 in the morning with a hymn and a prayer. Students had thirty minutes for lunch. Teachers dismissed classes at 2:30 in the afternoon. Wheelock prescribed daily exercises. These schools did not, as many African-American schools would later under the influence of Booker T. Washington, adopt the industrial principle. Instead, they offered a curriculum which provided African-Americans with an education competitive to whites. Furthermore, the curriculum focused on pupils' academic potential and offered basic elementary courses.[167]

Bureau schools operated day and night to provide an education to working African-Americans. By July 1866 more than 1,000 African-Americans attended twenty-five Bureau schools throughout

---

[164] Eby, The Development of Education in Texas, 265-66.

[165] Alton Hornsby, Jr., "The Freedmen's Bureau Schools in Texas, 1865-1870," Southwestern Historical Quarterly 76 (April 1973): 397.

[166] James Kirkman, SAC, to Charles Griffin, Assistant Commissioner (AC), Galveston, Texas, February 8, 1867; Vol. 48, pp. 137-38, Report of Operations, BRFAL, RG 105, NA.

[167] James W. Smallwood, "Education in Reconstruction Texas: The Contributions of the Freedmen's Bureau and Benevolent Societies," East Texas Historical Journal 19 (January 1981), 18-19.

Texas. The schools enrolled over 5,000 students by 1867. Approximately 40% African-American children received an education.[168]

As school enrollment increased, the Bureau reported freedpeople appeared anxious to obtain knowledge, and freedwomen engaged in activities to generate financial contributions to help support the schools. In addition to contributing funds earned from employment, freedwomen assisted the men and brought land, built either a church or school, and located teachers, whom they supported with tuition payments and presents, including food gathered at harvest.[169]

African-Americans who had received some education often worked as teachers in the early schools and taught what they had learned about reading, writing, and arithmetic. African-American women and men attempted to secure an education for themselves and for their children by buying primers and writing slates. Freedpeople contributed to their education as much as their resources allowed, and only then appealed for help from the Bureau.[170] The freedpeople's schools in Austin were "entirely self-supporting." Local African-American women and men gave money liberally; they "authorized one hundred in specie and another fifty to support the school. Due to their efforts, the school remained open."[171]

---

[168] Michael Allen White, "History of Education in Texas, 1860-1884" (Ed.D. diss., Baylor University, 1962), 213-16; John A. Edwards, "Social and Cultural Activities of Texans During Civil War and Reconstruction, 1861-1873" (Ph.D. diss., Texas Tech University, 1985), 137-38; J. W. Alford, Third Semi-Annual Report of Schools for Freedmen (Washington, D.C., 1867), 27-28; Alvord, Tenth Semi-Annual Report of Schools for Freedmen (Washington, D.C., 1869), 37-38; For information on education for freedpeople on local levels see J 3' 'allwood, Time of Hope, Time of Despair: Black Texans During Reconstruction (Port Washington, New York: Kennikat Press, 1981), 68-92.

[169] Smallwood, Time of Hope, Time of Despair, 27.

[170] Ibid., 85-86.

[171] Mrs. Fannie Campbell to George Whipple, Austin, Texas, November 24, 1866, American Missionary Association (AMA), Archives with References to Schools and Mission Stations, microfilm at the University of Maryland at College Park, Maryland. Hereinafter these records will be documented as AMA.

In spite of the financial contributions of freedpeople, the Bureau remained at the forefront in assisting them with their educational goals. The Bureau rather than state or local governments provided the first educational opportunities for African-American children in Smith County. It proposed furthering the education of the freedpeople by furnishing teachers and paying them a small salary, "so as to allow the indigent to attend school free of charge."[172] According to Frances Ellen Watkins Harper, an African-American female writer and orator, African-American women made many sacrifices and took various employment to "enable children to attend school, and they worked hard so the children would not have to take time away from school."[173] Harper emphasized this because a great portion of African-American children could not attend school due to poverty.

The Bureau also established schools with income generated from the Refugees and Freedmen's Fund. It decided free schools with limited tuition could only exist in cities and towns so they could "more immediately be under the supervision of the Bureau, and reach the greater number of children."[174] According to Wheelock, "the freedmen paid tuition and books; and, the teachers pay is supplemented by a small monthly sum, sufficient to defray the tuition of those who are too poor to pay the stipulated fee."[175] Another percentage of the teachers

---

[172] Gregory Barrett, SAC, to Charles Vernon, SAC, Tyler, Texas, June 30, 1868; Vol. 162, p. 187, Letters Sent, BRFAL, RG 105, NA, Washington, D.C.

[173] Gerda Lerner, ed. Black Women in White America: A Documentary History (New York: Random House, 1972), 246; See Harper's comments in "Colored Women of America," Englishwoman's Review 15 (January 1878), 65-68.

[174] Report of Brevet Major General J. B. Kiddoo, Assistant Commissioner for Texas, for the year ending December 31, 1866, p. 3, BRFAL, RG 105, NA, Washington, D.C.

[175] Report of Brevet Major General J. B. Kiddoo, Assistant Commissioner for Texas, for the year ending December 31, 1866, p. 8, BRFAL, RG 105, NA.

pay came from a "school fund" accruing from the sale of confiscated and abandoned property."[176]

In the Austin area, the free school had an estimated one hundred students, and "more than half that number had been turned away." At the same time the number of teachers at the paying schools had increased." Freedpeople assumed responsibility for providing education at the paying schools.[177]

In May 1866, Owen F. Baker, a federal appointee, opened a day school for freedwomen, men, and children in Marshall. It was not necessarily free; students who could afford to elected to pay a tuition of $1.50 per month. Baker's monthly reports to Edwin Wheelock, Superintendent of Education for Texas, showed an increase in attendance from 47 pupils in May to 149 by July 31. Attendance at the Sunday School reached more than 500, and Baker was assisted then by seventeen freedmen who could read. The number of students declined during the late summer and fall, possibly due to the need for labor in the cotton fields. Shortly thereafter, the school suspended operations completely in November and December.[178]

Many African-American schools survived due to the combined efforts of the Bureau, American Missionary Association, the freedpeople, and religious denominations. In 1867, the Bureau made arrangements with the American Missionary Association to furnish and pay teachers at a rate of fifteen dollars per month (Figure 4.2). It had a policy to pay only necessary expenses after the freedpeople had done their best with their own contributions. "This free school system, as it is called, is not designed to relieve the negroes from doing

---

[176] William Pease, SAC, to Joseph Reynolds, AC, Houston, Texas, July 23, 1867; Vol. 102, p. 113, Letters Sent, BRFAL, RG 105, NA, Washington, D.C.

[177] James Kirkman, SAC, to Charles Griffin, AC, Austin, Texas, February 8, 1867, Letters Sent, BRFAL, Vol 48, pp. 137-38, RG 105, NA, Washington, D.C.

[178] Owen F. Baker, Agent to Edwin Wheelock, Superintendent of Education for Texas, Austin, Texas, May 31, June 30, July 31, August 31, November 30, 1866; MC-822, n. p., Monthly Reports, BRFAL, RG 105, NA.

all they can themselves," a report explained, but "their means will be added to the . . . public help, and thus greatly enlarge, as well as perfect the general plan for their education."[179] Thus, the Bureau established "self-sustaining or pay schools."[180] The cost to attend these schools forced some African-Americans to take initiatives to acquire funds to pay for their education and establish their own schools. Therefore, although African-Americans received assistance from the Bureau and the American Missionary Association, they organized an unspecified number of schools on their own. Wheelock stated "from the first these schools were wholly supported by freedpeople."[181] General Joseph B. Kiddoo, who succeeded General Edgar Gregory as Assistant Commissioner of the Freedmen's Bureau, implied that whites would not oppose education for African-Americans if African-Americans were taught by other African-Americans. According to historian Jesse Dorsett, "he accordingly set out to provide as many black teachers as possible."[182] Superintendent of schools in Texas, Edwin Wheelock also supported the use of African-American female and male teachers throughout Texas: "I am also desirous during the existence of the Bureau, to get a number of colored people, of both sexes, prepared for teachers, so that they may assist in education and elevation of their own race . . ."[183]

A very popular newspaper, Flake's Bulletin, opposed education for African-Americans, but realized if Texas whites did not establish schools

---

[179] Report of Brevet Major General J.B. Kiddoo, Assistant Commissioner for Texas, for the year ending December 31, 1866, p. 2, BRFAL, RG 105, NA; Alvord, Third Semi-Annual Report on Schools for Freedmen, January 1, 1867, 27; Claude Elliott, "The Freedmen's Bureau in Texas," Southwestern Historical Quarterly 56 (July 1952), 11-13.

[180] First Report of Major General J. B. Kiddoo, July 23, 1866, p. 4, BRFAL, RG 105, NA.

[181] Report of Superintendent of Education for Texas, E. M. Wheelock, for the year ending December 1865, p. 3, BRFAL, RG 105, NA.

[182] Jesse Dorsett, "Blacks in Reconstruction Texas, 1865-1877" (Ph.D., Texas Christian University, 1981), 125.

[183] Report of Edwin M. Wheelock, Superintendent of Schools, October 31, 1866, Galveston, MIC-822, RG 105, NA, Washington, D.C.

for the freedpeople, then the federal government would establish them. By now, blacks and the Bureau had well established schools to educate blacks. However, on February 10, 1867, the newspaper "voiced widespread white southern suspicion of northerners" attempting to establish additional schools for African-Americans in Texas. It further "suggested what might be done . . . [besides teaching the freedman to says his a b c's, these teachers from abroad might put foolish notions in his head, and destroy the usefulness of his labor . . .] every planter who can find on his place a white or black person, intelligent enough to teach reading and writing, will avoid a world of perplexity by establishing the school and by not waiting for the government to send one who may perhaps inculcate notions not exactly in accordance with our social customs, and with the necessities of our situation."[184] In short, destroy the notion that blacks should be forever subservient.

It is questionable if these statements had some impact upon white attitudes toward education for African-Americans, because few whites took action to help establish schools for African-Americans. Furthermore, the problem of northern teachers in African-American schools was still "far from solved," because they still encountered threats from southern whites who opposed education for the freedpeople. Therefore, African-American teachers had to replace many northern white teachers who had been forced to resign. Also, the black community preferred African-American teachers because they believed that African-American teachers would show more interest in the students. Some African-Americans employed to teach in various places in the state had a local background and had obtained a "degree of elementary knowledge; a few were included among the "Yankee teachers" sent down by northern missionary societies."[185] In Houston, Miss Watson, an African-American, replaced Stuart, a white northern teacher who had been forced to leave the area. Before Stuart left, he

---

[184] Flake's Bulletin, Feb. 10, 1867.
[185] U. S. Bureau of Refugees, Freedmen, and Abandoned Lands, Third Semi-Annual Report on Schools for Freedmen, January 1, 1867 (Washington, D.C., 1867), 27.

had collected only the school tuition for the month. Therefore, the following month's tuition was due. However, most of the parents "refused to send their children to school unless Miss Watson would teach their children without fees." The trustees of the church in the meantime wanted twenty dollars rent for the month and expected her also to teach the remainder of the month without pay. She refused such a request, and as a result, she only retained six or seven students. Furthermore, the trustees of the church voiced dissatisfaction with Miss Watson and told her "she must vacate." They later replaced her with a freedman named Goodwin. She immediately contacted agent Byron Porter who sent word to the trustees that Miss Watson "should not be interfered with as she was teaching the school by your orders" and that she "would hold possession of the building until you could be heard from." Maybe, the trustees wanted an African-American male teacher because they thought the school would be more properly conducted under a male. They later persuaded Miss Watson to become an assistant teacher under Goodwin or Goodman.[186] So, although an African-American replaced a white northern teacher, gender conflict still persisted over African-American teachers.

The Bureau continued to carry out its intentions to use African-American teachers in Houston, Tyler, Marshall, and in other towns throughout Texas. Therefore, freedmen schools located in Texas were supplied with African-American teachers permanently located in Texas.[187]

The Bureau also provided schoolhouses for the freedpeople. According to Bentley, "a major demand was for buildings, not buildings rented or repaired, but schoolhouses built from the ground up and secured to the Negroes forever." To meet this need, the

---

[186] Byron Porter, Agent, to Edwin Wheelock, Superintendent of Education, July 21, 1866, Houston, Vol. 10, pp. 247-49, RG 105, NA, Washington, D.C.

[187] Report of Brevet Major General J. B. Kiddoo, Assistant Commissioner for Texas, for the year ending December 31, 1866, p. 3-4, Letters Sent, BRFAL, RG 105, NA.

assistant commissioners in most states acquired funds for buildings African-Americans began to construct. Theoretically they required them to do all they could, then came to their assistance and paid for completion of the buildings. In practice, they sometimes specified in advance how much of the construction African-Americans had to complete, before they would finish the buildings.[188]

Encouragement of this nature prompted the freedpeople of Georgia, for example, to acquire school buildings for black education in the state. The Bureau superintendent of education had reported in September 1867 that they had secured land in all quarters of the state. Freedwomen worked with the men to locate land for the schools. Some of it had been purchased by freedpeople themselves and some of it by northern societies, while other plots had been given to the them by individuals and city councils. Urgent appeals came in for Bureau assistance in building schoolhouses. They badly needed schools, said the superintendent, "for the African-American scholars of the state had advanced beyond the stage where church accommodations" would meet their school requirements. He had made "a kind of general promise" that wherever the people could secure land, he would help them, and would agree to pay their share toward the support of a school."[189] Texas instituted a similar program to encourage African-Americans to build and support their own schools. While the Bureau encouraged the building of schoolhouses, it continued to recruit African-American teachers.

To further promote education for African-Americans, the Bureau made arrangements with the American Missionary Association to furnish teachers for the state. Missionary schools sought to employ African-American students as teachers.[190] The Society agreed to support

---

[188] George R. Bentley, A History of the Freedmen's Bureau (New York: Octagon Books, 1970), 172; Report of Charles Griffin, Assistant Commissioner for Texas, Monthly Report, August 31, 1867, Box 39, n. p., Letters Received, BRFAL, RG 105, NA.

[189] George R. Bentley, A History of the Freedmen's Bureau (New York: Octagon Books, 1970), 172.

[190] Doss, Harriet E. Amos, "One Aspect of 'Domestic Reconstruction': Women's Missions to Former Slaves in Alabama During Reconstruction,"

teachers at African-American schools, and pay them fifteen dollars per month.[191] Miss Evans had been appointed to assist in the Austin school. She had been assigned to Miss Campbell at Austin. Furthermore, Miss Campbell had been advised to accept her, and if not she "was to be relieved and the school turned over to Miss Evans."[192] Miss Evans assumed control of the school and hired two African-American female assistants. Freedwoman, Luana Higgleston, a pupil of Miss Evans, worked as teaching assistant. Because she did such a fine job, Miss Evans "recommended that she be employed as an assistant teacher at ten dollars per month."[193] She reported that Laura Higgleston, "appeared to be fully competent in her capacity as an assistant teacher, and her services will be required as soon as the new school is completed."[194] Miss Evans also hired Amanda Robinson, an African-American female, as an assistant teacher. Amanda replaced Miss Evans and served as a teacher for all of the students. She taught day and Sabbath schools.[195]

In Marshall, Texas, Bureau agent Sweeney attempted to hire African-American teachers when efforts to promote education for blacks "had been rather cramped by the interference in an indirect manner of outside parties, and the teachers were woefully deficient." Yet after exhausting every effort, Sweeney had failed to get a decent boarding place for a good teacher and consequently had refrained from asking for one, therefore he focused his efforts on black education in Jefferson, Texas. He worked hard to establish a good school in Jefferson, and thought he

---

Southern Historical Association Meeting, November 12, 1993, Orlando, Florida.

[191] Report of Brevet Major General J. B. Kiddoo, for the year ending December 31, 1866, p. 2, BRFAL, RG 105, NA, Washington, D.C.

[192] James Kirkman, SAC, to Charles Griffin, AC, March 18, 1867; Vol. 46, n. p., Letters Sent, BRFAL, RG 105, NA.

[193] John Richardson, Agent, to James Kirkman, SAC, Austin, Texas, March 31, 1867, Vol. 48, pp. 163-65; May 16, 1867, Vol. 47, p. 8, Letters Sent, BRFAL, RG 105, NA.

[194] Oakes to James Kirkman, SAC, Austin, Texas, April 30, 1867, Vol. 48, pp. 182-84, RG 105, NA, Washington, D.C.

[195] Edwin Gay, Agent, to Charles Vernon, SAC, July 31, 1868, Austin, Vol. 49, pp. 189, RG 105, NA, Washington, D.C.

would succeed, and so far as he heard, no feeling was expressed against it. In Jefferson he assisted freedpeople in locating "a good teacher," and he supplied their school with benches and desks.[196] Sweeney persuaded the authorities to rent a small building at fourteen dollars a month for the purpose of operating the school. He hired Thomas Younger, a young African-American male, and reported in December "he has started a school and now has nineteen pupils." Sweeney visited the school twice after it opened, and he complimented Younger's educational progress at the school.[197] Sweeney considered Younger a "very respectable young colored man . . . qualified to instruct in the elementary branches of education fully." Younger impressed Sweeney to the extent he decided against establishing another school in the area, and against providing for another teacher because "as long as Younger teaches there would not be employment for another." Although the Bureau did not make provisions for another African-American teacher

at the school, Younger still benefitted from the efforts of freedwomen in the area who supported black education.[198]

In spite of the educational accomplishments of freedpeople, they still needed additional financial support to operate the schools, and a large majority of Texas whites opposed paying taxes to support any schools, including schools for freedpeople. They refused to support their own schools rather than give any support to the African-American schools due to apprehensions that their schools might later accept freedpeople.[199] General Kiddoo reported, "the people of Texas have violent prejudices against the North being imported to teach the negroes; they do not consider it compatible with the dignity of the Southern character to teach them themselves,

---

[196] Henry Sweeney, AC, to C. S. Roberts, Agent, October 31, 1868, Jefferson; Vol. 116, pp. 10-11, Letters Sent, BRFAL, RG 105, NA, Washington, D.C.

[197] Ibid., December 11, 1868, Vol. 116, p. 23.

[198] Henry Sweeney, AC, to Joseph Welch, Superintendent of Schools, December 12, 1868, Monthly Report, p. 23-24, RG 105, NA.

[199] William R. Davis, The Development and Present Status of Negro Education in East Texas, 135.

but are willing and anxious to have them taught by their own race." He proposed to take them at their word, and provided as many African-American teachers he could for that purpose. He believed "it would have the double effect of emulation among the colored people, and disarming the white people of one cause of prejudice against the efforts of the bureau."[200] Therefore, the Bureau intended to use African-American female and male teachers to suppress white opposition. In spite of this, interference from whites continued to hamper education for freedpeople. A report from Captain Stephen McCreecy, a Bureau agent, stated: "Many of the school planters will not allow schoolhouses on their places, or suffer their colored children to go to school. Where we have schools we experience great difficulty in sending letters and documents to our teachers. Sulphur Springs, Hopkins County, Texas is a place of this character. In that place there are now twenty widows and seventy-five orphan children, whose husbands and fathers have been murdered since the close of war. We wrote in vain to our teacher there; our letters were never given him. The teacher, a white male, after leaving the school, came "hither and reported the above facts."[201] Thus, many whites continued to oppose education for African-Americans, and to interfere with the educational efforts of freedwomen and freedmen.

Even the Texas State Teachers Association voiced opposition to education for freedpeople led by northerners and the Bureau, because it feared the influences of both might cause integration and social equality.[202] To make matters worse, most white Texans refused to teach in Bureau schools and would not rent rooms, or associate with northern teachers or Bureau officers affiliated with African-American

---

[200] Alvord, Third Semi-Annual Report on Schools for Freedmen, January 1, 1867, p. 28.

[201] William T. Clark, Children's Rights—Schools for All: Speech Delivered in the House of Reps, February 8, 1871 (Washington: F. & J. Rives and G.A. Bailey, 1871), 4.

[202] Texas State Teachers Association, Proceedings of the Texas Teachers' State Convention . . . 1866 (Louisville: John P. Morton and Co., 1866), 7.

education.[203] Furthermore, they often threatened northern white teachers and forced many of them to leave the state.[204]

As a result of increased white opposition, many schools became wholly supported by freedwomen and men.[205] Furthermore, they assumed responsibility to provide education for themselves because the state refused to accept responsibility to educate them, and assistance from other sources had decreased. Beginning in 1867, to educate themselves, freedwomen and freedmen throughout Liberty County established Sunday schools despite the failure of their crops which "last year left them in rather destitute condition so far as commanding ready money concerned."

They still managed to establish in the county, four day and night schools. Furthermore, "the progress amongst pupils is perfectly wonderful." The freedpeople had made these accomplishments because they had "solicited from their friends in the North, donations of Sunday school books with a promise that if they make a crop this year, they will subscribe liberally toward building a church sustaining them, for education purposes."[206]

African-Americans in Marshall established two of the five schools located in Harrison County. The Freedmen Fund and School Fund had accumulated by a total of $1199.50 by January 1867, a remarkable amount for black education.[207]

[203] Alwyn Barr, Black Texans: A History of Negroes in Texas, 1528-1971 (Austin: Jenkins Publishing Co., 1973), 61.

[204] Joe M. Richardson, Christian Reconstruction: The American Missionary Association and Southern Blacks, 1861-1890 (London, Athens: University of Georgia Press, 1986), 202-204.

[205] Report of the Assistant Commissioner for Texas, for the year ending 1866, Report of Brevet Major General J. B. Kiddoo, for the year ending October 31, 1866, p. 7, BRFAL, RG 105, NA, Washington, D.C.

[206] David L. Montgomery, SAC, to James Kirkman, SAC, Tyler, Texas, May 15, 1867, Vol. 140, p. 2-4, Letters Sent, BRFAL, RG 105, NA, Washington, D.C.

[207] Charles Rand, SAC, to Charles Garretson, Agent, Marshall, Texas, May 15, 1867; Vol. 134, n. p., Letters Sent, BRFAL, RG 105, NA.

In 1867, Marshall had one school building for African-Americans, and the rent cost twenty dollars per month. Even with this amount of rent to pay, freepeople still managed to sustain their school. At this school, Caroline Poe, an African-American female, and African-American male, William Massey taught from late 1867 into early 1869. Their reports for June, 1868, showed 123 pupils enrolled, and the monthly total remained approximately 100 for the rest of the year.[208]

In 1869, freedman Massey taught in Marshall until he was replaced on April 1 by L. J. Gallant, a white man from Indiana. Gallant insisted that local freedmen could not pay enough to support his school properly, therefore he asked the Bureau for a salary, but Massey and Caroline Poe had never received one. Gallant finally accepted in June a salary of fifteen dollars per month, although he wrote, "permit me to say we had been under the impression that Marshall could sustain a school for blacks." Gallant replied, "this place ought to support a school, but it does not do it. The people are less concerned about the education of their children than any place that I have been since the war." However justified, it appears unlikely that this attitude helped the situation. Gallant's last report for July showed fifty children enrolled and an average daily attendance of thirty-eight.[209]

At the end of February in 1869, Caroline Poe quit teaching for the Bureau, leaving only Massey's school with an enrollment of sixty-five students.[210] Evidently student enrollment dropped after both African-American teachers left. Maybe enrollment dropped because the students preferred African-American teachers who had shown more interest than Gallant in their education.

Occasionally agents commented that some African-Americans showed a lack of interest in education. However, it appears that the

---

[208] Monthly Reports, Caroline Poe and William Massey, June 1868, MIC-822, RG 105, NA, Washington, D.C.

[209] Assistant Superintendent of Education, Louis W. Stevenson, Monthly Report, April 1869, MIC-822, RG 105, NA, Washington, D.C.

[210] Caroline Poe and William Massey, Monthly Reports, February 1869, MIC-822, BRFAL, RG 105, NA.

occasional lack of interest existed because some African-Americans probably did not have enough funds to cover tuition expenses. Therefore, they probably lost interest in education since it seemed impossible without adequate revenue. Obviously, they needed money to support the schools and to supply it with teachers. On the other hand, maybe severe circumstances accounted for this lack of interest among some African-Americans, because sometimes night schools still flourished during heavy work seasons even when students had to work in the fields or outside the fields. They still maintained an interest in education although they had been "overreached on every hand" in the past years.[211] African-Americans continued to pursue an education regardless of work demands, money problems, and white opposition to education. Most importantly, freedwomen maintained a significant role in educational efforts.

African-American women not only taught school, but they enrolled in school at a much higher rate than men. In 1870, Harrison County in East Texas, had a total of 687 pupils attending school. More females of both races had enrolled at a higher rate than males, for example, 292 white females versus 283 white males, and fifty-nine African-American females had enrolled versus 53 African-American males. In comparison, in Smith County, 830 pupils enrolled in school. Less white females, than whites males attended school, 394 and 398 respectively, whereas, more African-American females than African-American males enrolled, twenty-seven and eleven respectively. Smith County in 1870 had seventy-two African-American schools with $20,000 in funds. By the end of 1872, the Bureau had discontinued all educational efforts for freedpeople in other counties in Texas, therefore African-American enrollment decreased for some time thereafter.[212]

---

[211] David L. Montgomery, SAC, Tyler, to I. P. Kirkman, Superintendent of Education, Galveston, Texas, July 31, 1867; Vol. 162, p. 37, Letters Sent, BRFAL, RG 105, NA>

[212] Bureau of the Census, <u>Ninth Census, The Statistics of the Population of the U.S.: Compiled from the Original Returns of the Ninth Census,</u> June

The Bureau finally had to seek support from white citizens to continue schools for freedpeople. Some property holders in Texas rejected the idea they should finance African-American schools. Property holders such as Judge John Hancock vehemently rejected supporting schools for freedpeople. He stated at a Democratic meeting in Texas: "Of all the wicked schemes ever devised by the wit of knaves to tyrannize over the people, to subjugate them soul, body, and State, and to rob them of their property for the enrichment of a worthless horde of strolling mendicants, this abominable school system seems to be the most complete.'"[213]

After the Bureau ceased educational operations in 1872, Republican legislators established a state school system for whites and African-Americans. However, African-American women and men still depended upon their own resources and contributions to sustain their schools because some whites still did not want them to have an education. But, despite such opposition, freedpeople with freedwomen at the forefront, continued to push for education because they realized they needed it to enable them to improve their condition. Having an education, learning to read and write, made them better citizens prepared to take control of their lives and to guide their families in meeting challenges brought about due to Reconstruction. Freedwoman, Annie Smith, an educator in Van Zandt, taught classes in the local community. She advised women to send their children to school to improve themselves.[214]

A few African-American female teachers had successful husbands, and they still continued to work as educators. African-American female educator, Mrs. Jessie Warren of Smith county was married to one of Smith county' leading African-American citizens, a middle-class businessman

---

1, 1870 (Washington, D.C.: Government Printing Office, 1872), 430; W. A. Redwine, Brief History of the Negro in Five Counties, 12.

[213] Austin Democratic Statesman, August 3, 1871.

[214] W. A. Redwine, Brief History of the Negro in Five Counties (Tyler: n. p., 1901); reprint, Chronicles of Smith County, Texas 11 (Fall 1972), 77.

Another female educator, Mrs. Mitchell, had a husband with a prominent business in the local community. she still worked as an educator, and became one of Tyler's leading educators. She was "one of the best experienced county teachers."[215]

Through the efforts of African-American women like Jessie Warren and Mrs. Mitchell, freedpeople demonstrated determination to exercise their right to have an education, and in some instances they taught themselves how to read and write. They also had an important role in the education process in the African-American community by especially providing guidance and educational support to their children. In Smith county, Marian Earthman educated her children. Due to her perserverance, her daughter became a teacher, and ranked "among the best teachers in Smith county." In Tyler, Mrs. Polly supported her childrn's quest for an education, and as a result, they also became teachers.[216]

It was essential for African-American women to support and promote education, and at the same time, maintain the black family, and the Bureau enabled them to deal with these concerns. Most important, the black family needed as much assistance as possible, and it appears that women, in addition to the Bureau, understood that having an education would make it easier for the survival of the black family and the black community. Thus, both accomplished important goals in education that assisted in the reconstruction of the black family.

---

[215] Ibid., 36.
[216] W. A. Redwine, <u>Brief History of the Negro in Five Counties</u>, 33

CHAPTER 7

Substaining The Family:
Labor and Freedwomen, 1865-1872

Jennie V. Parker, lived with her grandparents Jennie and Mitchell Allen throughout her childhood and recalled their memories of events in Clarksville, Texas, following emancipation. "I'll take care of my own grandchildren before I'll let someone else take them," vowed Jennie Allen, a freedwoman in Clarksville, Texas. With the assistance of her husband, Mitchell Allen, she raised three grandchildren while laboring as a sharecropper. As a result of joint efforts with her husband and assistance from African-American women in the community, Jennie provided a secure home for her children and grandchildren. African-American women in the community often babysat for Jennie and helped her with household chores when she had to work in the field during harvest time. Jennie always reminded her children how difficult slavery times had been for her as a child. She thanked God her life had improved since emancipation and that her children would have greater advantages. She was determined to improve their conditions by laboring outside the household and assuming responsibility for her family.[217]

---

[217] Jennie V. Parker of Ft. Worth, Texas, interview by author, 14 November 1991, tape recording, Residence, Cisco, Texas. Jennie V. Parker is the granddaughter of Jennie Allen. She lived with Jennie and Mitchell Allen

A raging debate exists about how many African-American women labored in the fields. Research shows that a majority of African-American women, like Jennie, assumed labor duties commensurate with their new status. They did this by utilizing the services of the Freedmen's Bureau. From the beginning the Bureau performed diverse duties. It served as a "labor clearinghouse, employment agency, and adjudicator of labor relations." In the local counties in East Texas, the Bureau largely assumed duties and responsibilities carried out during the war by the army and by civilian missionary and relief organizations. As historian Eric Foner has pointed out, the unifying mission of the bureau was to create in the South the foundation for a free society of labor: "one in which blacks labored voluntarily, having internalized the values of the marketplace, while planters and civil authorities accorded them the rights and treatment enjoyed by Northern workers."[218]

The Bureau attempted to establish a stable labor system in Texas through the use of labor contracts. In November of 1865, Freedmen's Bureau agents certified labor contracts before they became binding; they aided freedmen by limiting their work days to ten hours, less for women, and required a 5 1/2 day work week. Incidentally, employers paid from $2 to $15 per month for male field hands and from $2 to $10 for female hands.[219]

To supervise the enforcement of labor contracts, Colonel H. Seymour Hall had used Marshall as a base for his work as a sub-assistant commissioner in East Texas. One of his first steps was to publish a

---

throughout her childhood and recalled their memories of events in Clarksville, Texas, following emancipation.

[218] Barry A. Crouch, "Hidden Sources of Black History: The Texas Freedmen's Bureau Records as a Case Study," Southwestern Historical Quarterly 83 (January 1980): 217; Leslie Ann Schwalm, "The Meaning of Freedom: African-American Women and Their Transition From Slavery to Freedom in Lowcountry South Carolina," Ph.D. diss., The University of Wisconsin-Madison, 1991; Eric Foner, Reconstruction: America's Unfinished Revolution, 1863-1877 (New York: Harper and Row, 1988), 143-44.

[219] Smallwood, Time of Hope, Time of Despair, 43.

circular urging African-Americans to uphold their labor contracts, be responsible, and earn for themselves. He assured them that they "had the same freedom and rights as other men, and no more."[220]

The circulars issued by the Bureau in Marshall and Tyler encouraged African-Americans to remain with their employers and to sign labor contracts which stipulated a lien on crops and designated wages. Therefore, many freedpeople followed the bureau's advice and "worked for a portion of the crop, one-third being the share promised in some instances, and one-half the crop with the freedman paying half the expenses of the plantation, and to cloth and subsist themselves." The Bureau believed the one-third agreement was better for the freedmen. The circular announced that freedmen absent from work for two consecutive days or five work days in a month were considered vagrant and would be prosecuted. African-Americans convicted on this charge would be forced to labor for their employers or assigned to Bureau agents who would find employment for them. In Tyler, Emily Jones was contracted by the Bureau to work as a domestic to Captain Jennings. He initially refused to pay Emily for her service. The Bureau made him pay her $4.50.[221]

Assistant Commissioner J. B. Kiddoo, recommended yearly contracts and established strict fines for anyone involved in contract breaking. Kiddoo ordered that anyone convicted of "enticing laborers away from their work pay a fine of from $100 to $500; that freed people enticed away pay from $5 to $25; and that freed people who voluntarily broke contracts pay a $50 fine." According to Smallwoood, Kiddoo recommended his field agents to encourage good work habits among the freed people. In order to do this, some Bureau agents published

---

[220] Edgar M. Gregory, Assistant Commissioner, Galveston, Texas, October 6, 1865; Circular No. 1, Vol. 9, n. p., General and Special Orders and Circulars Issued and Rosters, BRFAL, RG 105, NA.

[221] Edgar M. Gregory, Assistant Commissioner, Galveston, Texas, October 12, 1865, Circular no. 1; October 17, 1865, Circular no. 2, Vol. 9, n. p., General and Special Orders and Circulars Issued and Rosters; Emily Jones, freedwoman, vs. Captain Jennings, Tyler, Texas, March 29, 1867, Vol. 164, p. 4, Register of Complaints, BRFAL, RG 105, NA.

a "list of all African-Americans who violated labor contracts and asked other employers not to hire them."[222] Furthermore, the Bureau emphasized, "should freed people not fulfill their part of the contract, the same state laws applied to whites under similar circumstances will be applied to them."[223]

The Bureau attempted to enforce labor contracts in a hostile environment. White citizens' clashed with African-Americans despite equitable labor agreements, and the Bureau agents realized racially based violence threatened their efforts with freedpeople in the community. Bureau agent Rand in Marshall reported that freedpeople did not receive justice in Red River County. He stated that freedpeople could be whipped "as usual—that being in the contract." In addition, "a negro must sign, he dare not leave," and "may have been produced and presented to the freedmen showing the inevitable effect of trying to leave."[224] James Oliver, a white man, shot freedman Knowles for refusing to contract with him.[225]

In 1867, the Bureau found that whites in Harrison county, like other counties throughout East Texas, had serious difficulty abiding by the labor guidelines. Most whites thought of African-Americans as inferior and subservient. Galveston's white newspaper expressed the attitude many in Texas held toward the freepeople in terms of their labor. Flake's Bulletin reported, "the Negro is worthless . . . he cannot be made to produce as much as he consumes or destroys . . . in every aspect which has reference to the present or future well being of the whites of the South, it would be infinitely better if he were away . . . to every desirable progress he is an insuperable obstruction . . . his presence

---

222 James W. Smallwood, "Perpetuation of Caste: Black Agricultural Workers in Reconstruction Texas," 61 (January 1979): 11.
223 William Garretson, Agent, to Edward Webb, Agent, Matagorda, Texas, June 22, 1867; Box 43, Letters Received, BRFAL, RG 105, NA.
224 Charles Rand, SAC, to James Kirkman, SAC, Marshall, Texas, April 20, 1867; Vol. 134, n. p., Letters Sent, BRFAL, RG 105, NA.
225 Charles F. Rand, SAC, to Henry Ellis, SAC, Marshall, Texas, January 10, 1867; Vol. 134, p. 4, Letters Sent, BRFAL, RG 105, NA.

Born in Slavery: Slave Narratives from the Federal Writers' Project, 1936-1938. Slave Narratives, Federal Writers Project, Manuscript Division, Library of Congress, Washington, DC.

is inimical, not merely to progress, but to safety . . . it is he by whom the famine is produced."[226] Such negative views resulted in increased violence toward the freedpeople. Historian Alwyn Barr attributed some white violence against the freedpeople to the "frontier nature of Texas society." He emphasized that terrorism in Texas seemed more prevalent than in other ex-Confederate states.[227] So African-American men and women had to contend with acts of violence along with labor problems.

Ignoring the fact that acts of violence against the freedpeople warranted Bureau intervention, a local newspaper in Marshall, The Harrison Flag, advised the Bureau to stay out of affairs concerning freedpeople. It reported, "the negroes are disposed to be contented, and if left to themselves would do much better for the country and their families than they do at present." After the renewal of the Bureau in 1867, prominent white men in the areas "declared illegal the Reconstruction laws, that the bureau had no authority, and that the people would be justified in resisting them."[228] However, based on popular attitudes, Bureau officials realized they needed to remain in the state to protect the civil and labor rights of the freed people. Freedwomen, like freedmen, accepted the Bureau's assistance in protecting civil rights, and they depended on the Bureau for labor assistance. They adjusted to freedom while at the same time they examined ways to provide a living for their family. One way they did this was by assuming paid labor outside the household. According to Jones, "women had to contend with the problem of finding and keeping a job . . . ."[229]

The interviews of elderly African-American women whose grandparents or great-grandparents lived during Reconstruction

---

226 Flake's Bulletin (Galveston), 1 January 1868.
227 Alwyn Barr, Black Texans: A History of Negroes in Texas, 1528-1971 (Austin: Jenkins Publishing Co., 1973), 43.
228 The Harrison Flag, 21 September 1867.
229 Jacqueline Jones, Labor of Love, Labor of Sorrow:Black Women, Work, and the Family From Slavery to the Present (New York: Basic Books, Inc., 1985), 53.

provide oral history accounts of the period reflecting freedwomen who had employment as early as their childhood days. The interviewee includes an eighty-one year old woman who provided information on the labor of her grandmother who as a child worked on a farm during Reconstruction in East Texas. The paternal grandmother, Josie Smith worked with her parents on "old man's Taylor's place." She picked corn, cotton, and bean crops.[230]

Freedwomen also established their own businesses as opposed to laboring in the fields. Bettie East, age ninety, and Lee Roberson, age eighty-four, described African-American women who had their own businesses during Reconstruction. Bettie remembered a woman her grandmother told her about named Mrs. Bertha, a widow who owned a grocery store. Everyone in the neighborhood in LaGrange shopped at her store because she had "good prices and some of the best baked goods." Lee Roberson told about a lady named Mrs. Haynes who operated an "eating place offering home cooked meals."[231]

Both women related how some married women had to work in the fields with their husbands to make a living. They mentioned a Hattie Blair, Jannie Kuykendell, and Ida Parker who worked on farms with their husbands in LaGrange.[232] They had little choice but to accept such labor because most owners of large plantations had adopted the system of tenancy or sharecropping which required the labor of all household members.[233]

Many African-American women performed housewifery chores—washing, ironing, keeping house, nursing children, cooking,

---

[230] Jennie V. Parker, interview by author, 14 November 1991, Ft. Worth, tape recording, residence, Ft. Worth, Texas.

[231] Bettie East, interview by author, 19 November 1991, 22 August 1992; Lee Robinson, interview by author, 20 November 1991, Cisco, tape recording, Cisco, Texas.

[232] Bettie East, interview by author, 19 November 1991, 22 August 1992, Cisco, tape recording, residence, Cisco, Texas; Lee Roberson, interview by author, 20 November 1991, Cisco, tape recording, Cisco, Texas.

[233] Carter G. Woodson, The Rural Negro, rpt., (New York: Russell and Russell, 1969), 45.

cleaning—as paid and unpaid laborers. After Ann Hawthrone's husband died, she washed and ironed and cooked out and raised her children. Sarah Cook stayed at home and took care of the children. Her husband, Nat Cook worked as a teamster. Not only did Sarah stay at home, but their daughter, Caroline stayed at home and took care of her seven year old son. According to Smallwood, freedwomen also supervised or did less strenuous farm work such as milling, feeding chickens and hogs, and gathering eggs. They sewed their own clothing; dried and preserved fruits and vegetables; made molasses and preserves; grew and picked fruits and vegetables; and, produced butter, candles, and soap, for their families.[234]

The labor contract policies of the Army and the Freedmen's Bureau attempted to give African-American men control over African-American women's labor. The Bureau held "men responsible for their wives unwillingness to labor according to a contractual agreement."[235] In many cases husbands and fathers signed for entire families. Furthermore, the Bureau instituted labor policies for the freedmen and women, with different guidelines for each. Although not surprisely, historian Leslie Schwalm maintains that family and gender relations, as well as labor relations, remained central to the efforts made by Bureau agents and military authorities to create a free labor society. Freedwomen in East Texas shared similar labor experiences to those of freedwomen in South Carolina. They had a crucial role in the transition to a free labor society in lowcountry South Carolina. South Carolina freedwomen participated in the struggle over the meaning of free labor. They responded to the "bureau's efforts to create a particular family model (and a particular role for women within the family) and make it one of the key (but unrecognized) building blocks of free labor society."

---

[234] Rawick, ed., The American Slave, Part 2, Vol. 4, 122 (Ann Hawthorne). U. S. Bureau of the Census, Population schedules, manuscript census returns, 1870, Clarksville, Texas; Smallwood, Time of Hope, Time of Despair, 47, 117.

[235] Jacqueline Jones, Labor of Love, Labor of Sorrow: Black Women, Work, and the Family from Slavery to the Present (New York: Basic Books Inc., 1985), 62; Dorothy Sterling, We Are Your Sisters: Black Women in the Nineteenth Century (New York: W.W. Norton, 1984), 328.

In Texas, similar to other former confederate states, the Bureau allowed planters to designate the husband the head of the household with responsibility for the labor of the entire family and the enforcement of labor contracts. Neil and Amanda Hamlin signed a labor agreement with John Hill, a prosperous farmer in Walker County. Neil's name appeared first on the contract agreement, and then his wife's name appeared with the terms specified for both. It appears that Neil had the initial responsibility to abide by the terms of the contract, whereas the planter had full control over both laborers. Terms for Amanda appeared more specific. It required her to "rise at the break of day and serve the said John Hill as seamstress, Milk Maid, washerwoman, or in any other capacity in which her services may be required." Furthermore, it required her "to milk and feed cattle on Saturday evenings and Sundays as on other days." Apparently, the employer attempted to place constraints on her labor by requiring her to work on days she should have had off to take care of her family needs. She probably had to comply with the terms of the contract because her husband had agreed to them.[236]

Discontented employers would complain when husbands failed to assume full responsibility for determining which family members would work, and for which planter. They also demanded African-American women and children to work alongside the men because they did not want African-American women to think they could act like white women by staying away from work in the field with men and children.[237]

Occasionally, East Texas African-American women resisted such interference from men when dealing with labor matters. They appeared

---

[236] Leslie Ann Schwalm, "The Meaning of Freedom: African-American Women and Their Transition From Slavery to Freedom in Lowcountry South Carolina," 290; John Hill to Neil Hamlin, 18 January, 1867, Hill Papers, Archives, University of Texas Library, Austin. John Hill (1826 [?]—1878), a prosperous farmer, owned three plantations in Texas. At his home plantation Old Waverly, near Waverly, Texas, he employed many freedmen and women.

[237] Jones, Labor of Love, Labor of Sorrow, 60; Sterling, We Are Your Sisters, 321-22.

more vocal than their husbands in asserting their rights in the work force. They would ask the Bureau to set aside unfavorable labor contracts their husbands had agreed to without their consent, or they would encourage their husbands to quit working for employers accused by them of unfair labor practices. Harriet Purnell went to the Bureau to protest a labor contract she and her husband had agreed to with a Mr. Brown. She asked the Bureau to allow them to be released from their contract with Mr. Brown because she said that he had failed to comply with the terms of the contract requiring him to pay each of them "ten dollars per month and furnish each of them three and a half pounds of Bacon and one peck of corn meal per week or its equivalent in other provisions." Furthermore, she requested the Bureau to make Mr. Brown pay them their past due wages amounting to $100. The Bureau dismissed this case because all parties failed to appear. In another case, Betsy Scott sued James Thompson for "refusing to pay for services for herself and her husband in 1867." Thompson had to pay her three dollars.[238]

The agents' experience at settling labor disputes between employers and laborers caused Bureau officials to contemplate the types of contracts they should encourage between freedpeople and planters. In the fall of 1866, Assistant Commissioners Wood, Ord, and Kiddoo favored crop-sharing contracts for the freedpeople, but Assistant Commissioner Scott had concluded that a money-wage system was better.[239]

Many employers refused to abide by the terms of the labor contracts whether they had crop-sharing or money-wage terms. George Harnadge of Tyler refused to pay Milley Kennedy her one-third of the crop which he had agreed to in a written contract. Eliza Newsome of Marshall had worked as a cook for Thomas Darner and he had refused to pay her

---

[238] Harriet Purnell, freedwoman, vs. A. Brown, Tyler, Texas, June 24, 1868, Vol. 163, pp. 20-21; Betsy Scott, freedwoman, vs. James Thompson, Tyler, Texas, May 1, 1868, Vol. 163, pp. 12-13, Register of Complaints, BRFAL, RG 105, NA.

[239] George R. Bentley, A History of the Freedmen's Bureau (New York: Octagon Books, 1970), 150; General and Special Orders and Circulars Issued and Rosters, October 1, 1866; Box 336, BRFAL, RG 105, NA.

$150 he owed for her yearly wages. As a result, the Bureau made him pay her $111 as wages past due. Lucinda Jones who had been hired for a year at twenty dollars, never received her wages from John Pike. Both parties failed to appear for the hearing.[240] In Tyler, Thomas Swann failed to give Sarah Johnson her fair portion of the crop raised for the year.[241] Freedwomen continued to protest unfair compensation and accuse employers of cheating them out of their wages. Jane Coleman filed a complaint against her employer, Benjamin McFadden, who had failed to pay her and her husband their past due salary of fifteen dollars. McFadden admitted he owed them and agreed to pay.[242]

Many African-American women testified to the Bureau that employers often dismissed "them without pay as they neared the end of the contract year."[243] Sally Ross of Robertson County reported J. W. Marise for nonpayment of services rendered. She and her two children had a contract with Marise in 1867. Marise had paid them $20 in advances but still owed them $46. The Bureau canceled Sally's contract with Marise, and made him pay her what he owed her.[244]

Freedwomen opted for sharecropping which they believed offered better compensation and more control over their work than domestic labor. They also preferred sharecropping during Reconstruction because they wanted to work at home, with family members, as well as work

---

[240] Milley Kennedy, freedwoman, vs. George Harnadge, Tyler, Texas, April 8, 1867, Vol. 164, p. 10, Register of Complaints; Eliza Newsome, freedwoman, vs. Thomas Darner, Marshall, Texas, November 30, 1868, Vol. 136, p. 78; Lucinda Jones, freedwoman, vs. John Pike, Marshall, Texas, November 30, 1868, Vol. 136, p. 79, Register of Complaints, BRFAL, RG 105, NA.

[241] Sarah Johnson, freedwoman, vs. Thomas Swann, Tyler, Texas, December 17, 1867; Vol. 164, p. 101, Register of Complaints, BRFAL, RG 105, NA.

[242] Jane Coleman, freedwoman, vs. Benjamin McFadden, Tyler, Texas, March 10, 1868,; Vol 163, pp. 4-5, Register of Complaints, BRFAL, RG 105, NA.

[243] Sterling, We Are Your Sisters, 332.

[244] Sally Ross, freedwoman, vs. J. W. Marise, Robertson, Texas, September 13, 1867; Vol. 156, p. 27, Register of Complaints, BRFAL, RG 105, NA.

with female members and friends, in order to reinforce female bonds which strengthened their identity as women.[245]

Many freedwomen worked as sharecroppers, tenant farmers, or wage laborers in the field. They continued to labor in the fields on farms where sharecropping served as the primary mode of production. According to historian Joan Jensen, freedwomen "spent more time occupied in duties similar to those of Euro-American farm women." Freedwomen would be in nuclear family households assuming full responsibility and raising their own children rather than sharing or allowing older black women to take care of their children as they had during slavery. Therefore, sharecropping may have been more suitable for freedwomen than "working for wages in fields or towns," because they would have more time for their households. [246]

Freedwoman Sarah Wilson related how sharecropping worked. According to Wilson, the employer gave a specific amount of food and clothing in exchange for labor. Sharecroppers took care of the land and gathered the crops while the employer paid for their groceries, doctor bills, and medicine. They did not receive any pay for their labor. Instead, the employer would log in his book a fixed amount to pay the sharecroppers and in "dis here book dar's little pieces all printed an' fixed up, an' de share-cropper he trades dese here little scraps ob paper down at de plantation sto' fer what he gwine git . . . he can't go no whar else ter trade, only jes' on de plantation whar he makin' de crop. Dat ere way . . . he can't go git drunk an' sech but de ole woman an' de kids dey git somefin' dey needs."[247]

[245] Dorothy Sterling, ed. We Are Your Sisters: Black Women in the Nineteenth Century (New York: W.W. Norton, 1984), 331.

[246] Carolyn E. Sachs, The Invisible Farmers: Women in Agricultural Production (Totowa: Rowman and Allanheld, 1983),24-25; Joan Jensen, With These Hands: Women Working on the Land (Old Westbury: Feminist Press, 1981), 73.

[247] Rawick, ed., The American Slave: A Composite Autobiography. Supplement Series 2. Vol 6. Texas Narratives, Part 5, 4221-22 (Sarah Wilson).

Oftentimes, African-American women as well as African-American men felt compelled to work as sharecroppers because they had no other means of making a living, therefore sharecropping served as an alternative. The work East Texas African-American women performed in the fields consisted primarily of chopping and picking cotton, and hoeing corn. Lucy Thomas worked in the field, hoeing crops.[248] Martha Watkins picked cotton at the John McDougat plantation in Smith County. She had reported McDougat to Bureau officials for cheating her out of wages.[249]

Based on accounts of sharecropping, the freedpeople seemed barely better off financially than they had been as slaves. However, their working conditions may have improved; they had some control over their own labor and could specify their working hours, and a few managed to buy land.[250] In East Texas, Mary Hinton and Henriett Fleming lived together, and both worked as field laborers. Doshea Moore, worked as a farmer to assist her husband John who was also a farmer.[251]

Many women finding themselves unwilling to cope with sharecropping labor demands and restrictions placed upon them by white employers decided to work for themselves. African-American women realized the importance of land ownership in helping their family or kin. However, only a few African-American women managed to purchase land. As landowners, some African-American women hired family members to work as sharecroppers. Matilda Boozie Randon farmed and rented land to family members and other freed people. She labored on the farm, while

---

[248] Carolyn E. Sachs, The Invisible Farmer: Women in Agricultural Production (Totowa: Rowman and Allanheld, 1983), 25-26; Lucy Thomas, File 4H357, Marshall, Texas, Works Progress Administration Records, Center for American History, Barker History Collection, University of Texas, Austin.

[249] Martha Watkins, freedwoman, vs. John Mc Dougat, Tyler, Texas, December 11, 1868; Vol. 163, pp. 36-37, Register of Complaints, BRFAL, RG 105, NA.

[250] Sterling, ed., We Are Your Sisters, 331.

[251] U. S. Bureau of the Census, Records of the Bureau of the Census, Population Schedule, Ninth Census (1870), Tyler, Texas, RG 29, Washington, D.C.

A.M. Moore,
ex-slave in Marshall

*Born in Slavery: Slave Narratives from the Federal Writers' Project,
1936-1938.   Slave Narratives, Federal Writers Project, Manuscript
Division, Library of Congress, Washington, DC.*

her husband worked as a minister. She hired as sharecroppers her niece and husband. Matilda had acquired 1500 acres of land from her former master. She said that at the age of thirteen during slavery she was raped by her owner's son, and "bore his child." As a result, her former owner gave her this land upon emancipation.[252] Only a few African-American women who wanted to control their labor or have possession of their own land acquired such. Years later, to keep freedpeople as tenants, the "Landlord and Tenant Law of 1874 amended in 1876 prohibited tenants from sub-renting land without the consent of the landlord."[253]

Freedwomen without land in East Texas coped with poverty and financial hardship by laboring as field hands in male dominated field labor under adverse work conditions. In East Texas many white employers dismissed African-American women "who questioned their orders, behaved too independently, or spoke in the wrong tone sounding insolent or insubordinate." Moreover, in late summer, after the final cultivation of crops, the laborers, men and women, had little work to do until the next harvest. Therefore, planters often drummed up false charges against the freedpeople to justify driving them away without pay. Thereafter, the planters would replace them with other workers, thus minimizing their outlay for labor.[254] Planters knew it would be easy to replace African-American's labor, therefore their labor had little value. In many instances where freedpeople had worked for a portion of the crop, their entire portion had been "absorbed by "advances" made them during the year of articles of merchandise, not necessary for their maintenance or comfort, and at exorbitant prices—such as cheap jewelry, worthless ponies and intoxicating liquors." In such cases freedpeople, not seeing any material results from their labor, became more or less discouraged and unwilling to enter into contracts for the ensuring year.[255]

---

[252] Winegarten, Finder's Guide to the Texas Woman, 159.
[253] Pitre, Through Many Dangers, 71.
[254] Nieman, To Set the Law in Motion, 215-16.
[255] Joseph Kiddoo, Assistant Commissioner, to Oliver O. Howard, Commissioner, Galveston, Texas; Report of Bvt. Major General J.B.

Employers complained that freedpeople were lazy and did not want to work when they refused to enter into contacts for labor. The <u>Freedman's Press</u> responded to accusations by whites "about the freedmen would not work and had done so during slavery only because of the lash." It stated, "Oh, yes, replies the enemy of the freeman, that is all true, but he did all this under the whip, under the cutting lash of slavery." "That is true, but we contend that he will do still more than he has ever done before, the kind and generous hand of liberty." "The cry of 'the nigger wont work' is dying out; he is the only man who has worked as a rule in the South; he is the only man who has tilled the soil while his white neighbors have rammed their hands into their pockets and stood about the corners of the towns and villages mourning over the 'lost cause.'" "Black muscle had built up the South, now under freedom and under God, his muscle and brain will not only rebuild the wealth of the South, but build up a home for every colored man."[256]

White landowners devised ways to maintain control over the labor of freedwomen and men willing to make contracts. After they would convince the freedpeople to agree to a contract, they would try to trick them into remaining at their jobs to prevent them from engaging in sharecropping at another plantation. At the same time, they would try to cheat them out of their wages. David Cade tried to cheat Rachel Cooper by paying her $80 in greenbacks, which had no value, when he should have paid her in specie. He finally paid her $19.50. Unscrupulous masters would promise them full rations and a share of all crops; some would even promise to give them small plots of land and livestock. After the harvest, most employers would refuse to honor their agreements. Instead, they would run the freedpeople away from their property without paying any compensation.[257]

Kiddoo, for the year ending December 31, 1866.

[256] The Freedman's Press (Austin), "The Muscle of the Colored Man," July 18, 1868.

[257] James Butler, SAC, to David Montgomery, SAC, Tyler, Texas, July 12, 1867; Vol. 164, n. p., Register of Complaints, BRFAL, RG 105, NA.

In Jefferson, J. H. Smith drove Moses Letcher and his wife off his place without paying them for their labor.[258] William Garrett drove off Lucy Smith after she had worked four months without pay. The Bureau made him pay her $6.25 for past due wages.[259] Frost Kelley "turned out Jennie Fletcher and her children" and refused to pay her for seven months work. The Bureau ordered him to pay her $31.46 for past due wages.[260] J.T. Hand in Tyler, Texas refused to pay Charity Adkins. He was to have paid her twelve dollars for three months service at the rate of four dollars per month in 1865.[261] Frank Deshaugher refused to pay Harriet Daniels sixty dollars for services rendered. The Bureau summoned Deshaugher to appear before the court, but he never reported. The Bureau requested his arrest as soon as he was found. Ann Kirby reported that T.H. Davenport owed her twenty-four dollars for her work. Caroline Rosebud had worked as a cook for six months on Oscar Johnson's farm, and her wages had amounted to twenty-eight dollars. Johnson paid her only eight dollars and fifty cents, and then discharged her without paying the twenty dollar balance. The Bureau had to force Johnson to pay Caroline.[262]

All the above cases show that freedpeople constantly had to seek assistance in getting paid. In some instances, employers probably did not pay the freedwomen and men because they did not have cash after

---

258 Henry Sweeney, SAC, to Charles Roberts, SAC, Jefferson, Texas, October 31, 1868; Vol. 116, p. 4, Letters Sent, BRFAL, RG 105, NA.

259 Lucy Smith, freedwoman, vs. William Garrett, Tyler, Texas, May 1, 1868; Vol. 163, pp. 12-13, Register of Complaints, BRFAL, RG 105, NA.

260 Jennie Fletcher, freedwoman, vs. Frost Kelley, Tyler, Texas, November 16, 1867; Vol. 164, p. 90, Register of Complaints, BRFAL, RG 105, NA.

261 Charity Adkins, freedwoma, vs. J. T. Hand, Tyler, Texas, June 28, 1867; Vol. 164, p. 47, Register of Complaints, BRFAL, RG 105, NA.

262 Harriet Daniels, freedwoman, vs. Frank Deshaugher, Tyler, Texas, March 24, 1868, Vol. 163, pp. 4-5; Ann Kirby, freedwoman, vs. J. W. Davenport, Tyler, Texas, March 28, 1868, Vol. 163, pp. 6-7; Caroline Rosebud, freedwoman, vs. Oscar Johnson, Marshall, Texas, November 7, 1868, Vol. 136, p. 57, Register of Complaints, BRFAL, RG 105, NA.

the war, and some did not compensate them because they thought they could easily avoid paying without any repercussions.[263]

In addition to refusing to pay freedpeople for their labor, some white employers agreed not to hire them women because they feared that if they allowed them to move from one plantation to another, they might gain their independence, and therefore become more difficult to manage. Furthermore, they believed that if freedpeople gained their independence, they would demand more wages and play employers against each other. Therefore, "the policy of the late slave owners, who are forming combinations, is to prevent other persons from hiring the freedmen, until Winter approaches, so that, sheer necessity will compel them, to remain with their former masters without compensation."[264] According to the Bureau, the contracts generally gave much in "favour of the planter, not naming the obligations of the employer to as full extent as they should . . . the colored people are still mistreated in this county by people that have been classed with those of wealth."[265] Freedwomen showed their opposition to such conditions by refusing to labor as expected.

Evidence in the Texas Bureau records shows that freedwomen probably "resisted not work itself, but work in a form which undermined their independence and freedom." A young freedwoman named Lively had a habit of leaving her job without permission. She refused to allow her work to tie her down, so she would come and go as she pleased. Mary Boyce reported Lively's actions to the Bureau. It is unknown what action the Bureau took against Lively for failing to work as agreed upon.[266]

---

263 Barry A. Crouch, "Hidden Sources of Black History: The Texas Freedmen's Bureau Records as a Case Study," Southwestern Historical Quarterly, 83 (January 1980): 217.

264 Andrew Hamilton to H.G. Wright, September 27, 1865, Hamilton Papers, Texas State Library, Austin, Texas.

265 Charles Griffin, AC, Boston, Texas, August 31, 1867; Box 39, Monthly Report, pp. 1-2, BRFAL, RG 105, NA.

266 Crouch, "Hidden Sources of Black History," 222; Mary A. Boyce, white female, to Captain Shorkley, Agent, Clarksville, Texas, October 9, 1868;

The number of African-American women employed increased as they became more assertive and assumed more control over their lives [267] And, they still had to cope with labor contract guidelines established by the employers. The Bureau's wage guidelines mandated that African-American women and men receive unequal compensation based on their sex rather than their productive abilities or efficiency. In Limestone county, L.A. Stroud hired Elizabeth, the wife of Merritt Trammell, as a house woman at the rate of $5 per month with "one half to be paid in money and the other half in cotton cloth at the rate of 12 cents per yard."[268]

Freedwomen expressed mixed feelings toward the various labor contracts affecting their households and labor. Despite such misgivings, many freedwomen went back to work in the fields with their husbands to help provide necessary resources for the family, or until they could procure their own farm. In Tyler, Emma Taylor and her husband accepted work as farm laborers for thirty-five cents a day. They finally saved enough money to buy their own farm, then they went to work for themselves.[269] Freedwoman Hannah had always worked with her husband to help take care of the household. Hannah and her husband, Joseph worked together for Mr. Cameron who recommended them to be "honest and industrious persons."[270]

Not all freedwomen labored outside the household with their husbands. Those remaining at home still worked as field laborers. Historian Jacqueline Jones maintains that African-American women

---

Box 39, n. p., Letters Received, BRFAL, RG 105.

[267] James M. Smallwood, Time of Hope, Time of Despair: Black Texans During Reconstruction (Port Washington: Kennikat Press, 1981), 54, 115-17.

[268] Doris Pemberton, Juneteenth at Comanche Crossing (Austin: Eakin Publications, 1983), 54.

[269] Emma Taylor, 4J295, Tyler, Texas, Works Progress Administration Records, Center for American History, Barker History Collection, University of Texas, Austin.

[270] B. Cameron, white male, to, To Whom It May Concern, Henderson, Texas, January 8, 1867; Box 43, n. p., Letters Received, BRFAL, RG 105, NA.

Born in Slavery: Slave Narratives from the Federal Writers' Project, 1936-1938. Slave Narratives, Federal Writers Project, Manuscript Division, Library of Congress, Washington, DC.

also assumed domestic duties at home as wives and mothers. Amy Morris stayed at home and took care of the children ages five, three, and six months, while her husband Otis worked as a farmer. Elijah Darnell, a farmer with an estate valued at $500, had a wife named Angy who stayed at home and kept house while the men of the household worked in the field. Their sons, Joseph, Elijah, and Handy assisted in the farming tasks.[271]

Based on historian Jones' assertion, the "withdrawal of African-American women from wage labor—a major theme in both contemporary and secondary accounts of Reconstruction occurred primarily among the wives and daughters of able-bodied men." Elijah Darnell, a farmer in Clarksville, with a personal estate valued at $500, had a wife named Angy who stayed at home and kept house. While his sons, Joseph, Elijah, and Handy assisted him in farming. Mary Efferson stayed at home and cooked and cleaned for her family. Her husband, Dick worked as a farmer, along with their son Edy. Elizabeth Ludley's husband, Mason worked as a carpenter. Thus, he enabled Elizabeth to stay at home to take care of their five children. The youngest child was only two months old.[272]

In a few instances, African-American women refused to work in the fields and insisted on working in their own households, "and their husbands concurred in this view." On the other hand, many freedwomen had to accept work to support themselves and their children since they had to assume sole support for the household." Freedwomen who served as the head of household for their children or other family members "had to take work wherever they could find it." Rachel Whitfield, a subsistence farmer, made it on her own as head

---

[271] Jacqueline Jones, Labor of Love, Labor of Sorrow: Black Women, Work, and the Family From Slavery to the Present (New York: Basic Books, Inc., 1985), 63; White, Arn't I A Woman, 122; U. S. Bureau of the Census, Population schedules, manuscript census returns, 1870 Clarksville, Texas.

[272] Jones, Labor of Love, Labor of Sorrow, 58; U. S. Bureau of the Census, Population schedules, manuscript census returns, 1870, Clarksville, Texas.

of household. Elizabeth Hagerty served as the breadwinner for her family. Her employment as a housekeeper sustained the family and put restrictions on her time. Elizabeth's contract with her employer, L.A. Stroud, only allowed one-half of each Saturday to wash their own clothing. Elizabeth, advanced in pregnancy and with three children, tried to work to care for her children, but she received no wages, only food and clothing for her family. Martha Clark worked as a laborer for Lee Robinson. She requested a share of the crop for her services. She reported Robinson to the Bureau because he refused to pay her share of the crop. The records did not reveal the results of this case.[273]

In addition to laboring as field hands, freedwomen worked as domestics. The domestic work they performed as paid laborers consisted of cooking, cleaning, laundering, and sewing. They assumed such household labor to provide for their families. According to sociologist Robert Staples, freedwomen had to return to familiar jobs "working in the white man's kitchen." Betty Rodgers worked as a cook for Mr. Sutton, a retired lawyer in Clarksville. Sally Humphries worked as a cook for a dry goods merchant, Mr. Cheatham. In Tyler, Leona Washington worked as cook for the Vesey household.[274]

Freedwoman Julia Malone worked as a laundress. According to her, "I washes for de livin' and washes old massa's daughter's clothes."[275]

---

[273] Jones, Labor of Love, Labor of Sorrow, 58; Doris H. Pemberton, Juneteenth at Comanche Crossing (Austin: Eakin Publishing, 1983), 54-55; Ruthe Winegarten, Finder's Guide to the Texas Woman: A Celebration of History Exhibit Archives (Denton: Texas Woman's University, 1984), 200; Martha Clark, freedwoman, vs. Lee Robinson, Tyler, Texas, April 27, 1868; Vol. 163, pp. 12-13, Register of Complaints, BRFAL, RG 105, NA.

[274] Staples, The Black Woman in America, 15; U. S. Bureau of the Census, Population schedules, manuscript census returns, 1870, Clarksville, Texas; Center for American History, Barker Texas History Collection, Negro Scrapbook, "The Old Time Negroes Were Imbued With a Spirit of Loyalty Yet to Be Surpassed in These Times-Only a Few Still Live." n. d., University of Texas, Austin, Texas.

[275] Weiner, "Plantation Mistresses and Female Slaves,'" Rawick, ed., The American Slave, Part 3, Vol.5, 44 (Julia Malone).

Born in Slavery: Slave Narratives from the Federal Writers' Project, 1936-1938. Slave Narratives, Federal Writers Project, Manuscript Division, Library of Congress, Washington, DC.

Another laundress, Matilda Boozie Randon "earned money by selling butter and eggs," to supplement her income. According to Matilda's great-granddaughter, Annie Mae Hunt, "she earned money washing and ironing clothes for white families." Matilda would sometimes earn as much as twenty-five or thirty dollars. With her earnings she purchased "all kinds of clothes and food for her family and grandchildren." Another freedwoman named Lucy Wright worked as a laundress to make ends meet.[276] In Nacogdoches, Aunt Eliza Walker made rock candy to sell to the local townspeople, and she also worked as a laundress.[277]

African-American women with young children experienced difficulty in finding and keeping jobs as domestic servants because whites felt children might interfere with the servant's duties.[278] Therefore, single freedwomen with children took whatever work available as domestic servants, so they engaged in paid domestic and household labor outside their homes. The census records give the impression that women shared child care responsibilies while working outside the household. In Clarksville, Sarah Dickson took care of Rosie King's two children, Mary and Joseph, while Rosie worked as a domestic servant.[279] Manchy Caton worked as a domestic servant while Ann Caton stayed at home and took care of Richard and Mary, ages five and seven. Ann Brown stayed at home and did housekeeping work for the family, and at the same time, she took care of her daughter's son Charley. The daughter worked outside the household as a cook.[280]

---

[276] Ruthe Winegarten, Finder's Guide to the Texas Woman, 159; I Am Annie Mae, 19-21.

[277] Center for American History, Barker Texas History Collection, Negro Scrapbook. "The Old Time Negroes Were Imbued With a Spirit of Loyalty Yet to Be Surpassed in These Times—Only a Few Still Live." n. d., University of Texas, Austin, Texas.

[278] Marli Frances Weiner, "Plantation Mistresses and Female Slaves: Gender, Race, and South Carolina Women, 1830-1880," 299.

[279] U.S. Bureau of the Census, Records of the Bureau of the Census, Population Schedule, Ninth Census (1870), Clarksville, Texas, RG 29, National Archives, Washington, D.C.

[280] U. S. Bureau of the Census, Records of the Bureau of the Census, Population Schedule, Ninth Census (1870), Clarksville, Texas, RG 29,

Many freedwomen, as domestic servants, labored for "very low wages," or no wages, for white women and men.

In cases where they received no wages they would receive compensation in the form of room and board or rations.

It is unknown whether freedwoman Rosie King received compensation in this manner. Rosie worked as a domestic servant for Sarah Dickson who did not have a husband.

The records show that Sarah did not work outside the household because she had listed her occupation as "keeping house." However, she may have had some income because she had employed Rosie as a domestic servant. Otherwise, she could not have paid Rosie in wages without an income. Another freedwoman, Lizzie Scott also worked as a domestic servant. She had received six dollars in wages and rations which helped her to support her four children.[281]

Even though African-American women had to resort to domestic work, at least, "she was able to procure employment, whereas in many instances the man could not because domestic work required black women." But a price had to be paid by the African-American woman, because "she often suffered indignities, physical abuse, and extremely low or lack of wages."[282] Dr. Reid refused to pay Sara Harris for her labor, and he threatened her life.[283]

In Marshall, Robert Cox refused to pay Lucy Davis. He owed her twenty dollars for labor performed. The Bureau finally settled the case.[284]

National Archives, Washington, D.C.

[281] U. S. Bureau of the Census, Population schedules, manuscript census returns, 1870, Clarksville, Texas; Freedmen's Contracts with Adam Hope, 1866, File, Harrison County Historical Museum, Marshall, Texas.

[282] Staples, The Black Woman in America, 15.

[283] Sara Harris, freedwoman, vs. Dr. Reid, Tyler, Texas, April 11, 1867; Vol. 164, p. 15, Register of Complaints, BRFAL, RG 105, NA.

[284] Lucy Davis, freedwoman, vs. Robert Cox, Marshall, Texas, December 10, 1868; Vol. 136, p. 85, Register of Complaints, BRFAL, RG 105, NA.

Problems encountered in domestic paid labor probably caused a few African-American women to prefer work in the field with family members or husbands. However, most freedwomen probably preferred domestic work even if they

had to work for some employers whose nagging and fault-finding may have been unpleasant. For example, Fanny Ingram worked as a domestic for a cantankerous employer named Mrs. Barnes. Fanny had a dispute with Mrs. Barnes who mistreated her, so she violated her contract, left, and sought other employment.[285]

Due to the fact that freedwomen would eventually leave unfavorable employment, employers had to find ways to retain adequate labor due to high turnover. The freedpeople often left over labor disputes concerning non-payment, sometimes involving assault. George Tucker, a freedman, owed Mary O. Douglas, a freedwoman, $50 for received goods and money. Tucker had promised to pay the full amount and 10 percent interest, but he moved to Marshall before he could be forced to pay his debt. Mary never received payment. Henry Bullard, a white employer, refused to pay Tempy Fare who had worked on his farm. He then assaulted her when she demanded payment for her labor.[286]

To further control labor, the black code section on vagrancy laws said "that all common laborers who didn't contract for a year within 20 days, or as soon thereafter as practicable after January 1, would be considered and treated as vagrants."[287] The Bureau issued a statement implying that "the laws passed pertaining to vagrancy, apprenticeship,

---

285 Weiner, "Plantation Mistresses and Female Slaves," 299; Fanny Ingram, freedwoman, vs. Mrs. Barnes, Tyler, Texas, September 27, 1867; Vol. 164, p. 78, Register of Complaints, BRFAL, RG 105, NA.

286 Mary O. Douglas, freedwoman, vs. George Tucker, Tyler, Texas, April 17, 1868, Vol. 162, p. 134; Tempy Fare, freedwoman, vs. Henry Bullard, Tyler, Texas, April 10, 1867, Vol. 164, p. 13, Register of Complaints, BRFAL, RG 105, NA.

287 Bryon Porter, Agent, Henry Ellis, SAC, Austin, Texas, October, 9, 1866; Vol. 48, n. p., Cash Accounts Report, BRFAL, RG 105, NA; Crouch, "'All the Vile Passions:'," 27-28; Gammel, The Laws of Texas, 1822-1897, Vol. 5, 979, 1020-21.

guardianship, minors and labor, make no distinction of color, and if impartially applied, will work no injustice; but the evident intent of these laws is to partially re-enslave the freedmen, and their application thus far have been confined to them."[288]

The Bureau seemed correct in its assessment of the vagrancy and apprenticeship laws because a majority of those affected unjustly by these laws happened to be African-Americans. The Southern Intelligencer defended the state's vagrancy law included in the 1866 black code. It stated "the Vagrant Law of Texas, defines a vagrant as `an idle person without visible means of support, and making no exertion to obtain a support by an honest employment.'"

The law gave the Chief Justice and all the Justices of the Peace the authority" to order the arrest of all vagrants.

The order could be issued based on the affidavit of three credible householders in the county. If convicted of vagancy, the Magistrate had the authority to order the vagrant to be put "to work in such manner the county court may direct." Thereafter, the County court would assume responsibility for providing "for the employment of vagrants on roads, bridges or other public works." These regulations required labor for the first offense to last not longer than one week, and "for any subsequent offense not longer than three weeks, during which time the person is to be supported, and additional compensation allowed if deserving, at the discretion of the Court." The law gave the same authority over vagrants to towns and cities. It also provided for the person arrested as a vagrant to have a trial by jury comprised of twelve householders.[289]

There appears no evidence that if an African-American female vagrant did demand a trial by jury, that she would ever receive one. It appears the Bureau had to take action to insure the vagrancy laws would be enforced fairly. Agent Gregory Barrett had been directed by

---

[288] Report of Bvt. Major General J.B. Kiddoo, for the year ending December 31, 1866, BRFAL, RG 105, NA.
[289] Southern Intelligencer, November 9, 1867.

the Acting Commissioner of Texas to call on the civil authorities to enforce the provisions of the vagrant law.[290]

After the federal government phased out the Bureau in Texas, and reduced army units, the situation worsened for freedpeople. Disgruntled whites continued to drive freedpeople from their crops after harvest, and then simply announced that the "runaways" forfeited all wages or shares due.[291] Such events occurred until 1872, when the Bureau phased out all operations in Texas, with its educational efforts the last to benefit freedmen and freedwomen. In essence, freed people benefitted from having the Freedmen's Bureau in East Texas. The Bureau had protected the labor rights of freedmen and freedwomen. After its departure from Texas, some whites continued to abuse and cheat freed people out of their wages. Previously, freed people could have depended on the Bureau to intervene in their behalf to insure wage grievances would be settled. Thereafter, they had to depend on their own efforts without Bureau assistance. Overall, the relief the Bureau afforded freedwomen affected how they responded to labor demands, and enabled them to assume active roles in the workforce to take care of their families.

---

[290] Charles Roberts, SAC, to Gregory Barrett, SAC, Tyler, Texas, August 13, 1868; Vol. 161, n. p., Letters Received, RG 105, NA.

[291] Smallwood, Time of Hope, Time of Despair, 62-63.

CONCLUSION

African-American women in Texas during Reconstruction worked with the Freedmen's Bureau to assist the family with major challenges due to freedom. Then, they focused on meeting the needs of the family. Through the use of Bureau services, they aspired to meet educational, social, and financial demands. They established significant relations with Bureau agents which enabled them to benefit the African-American family. The family survived due to African-American women's will and perserverance in addressing family and labor matters. They worked with freedmen to accomplish essential goals necessary for survival. Moreover, they enabled the family to survive despite many obtacles.

African-American women's obligations as mothers, wives, and laborers caused them to have renewed understandings of their importance in the African-American communities. Their obligations interacted with the Bureau, and extended beyond the household into the community and workforce. Moreover, African-American women used the services of the Bureau to strengthen the family and the community. Thus, they were equipped to tackle social and economic demands placed upon them. If they perceived a need to earn money, they sought agricultural and domestic work to improve their lifestyles. If they perceived a need for education, they assisted in educational efforts. Most important, they often pushed for justice amidst discrimination and abuse in workforce. Due to their actions and the Bureau, African-Americans received some protection in society and the labor force.

In East Texas, African-American women who made the transition from slavery to freedom, tried to help those more unfortunate, and at the same time, they maintained the black family. Most important, they used the Freedmen's Bureau to assist them in accomplishing their goals and protecting their rights. The Bureau proved very important in the lives of freedwomen. In essence, African-American women's interactions with the Bureau showed how they worked to meet demands men, women, and children placed upon them. Thus, this study shows that African-American women substained the black family due to their efforts with the Freedmen's Bureau. In summary they made accomplishments and survived obstacles within and outside the family.

BIBLIOGRAPHY

Primary Sources

Alvord, J. W. <u>Semi-Annual Reports on Schools for Freedmen, January, 1867—January, 1870</u>, 10 Vols., National Archives, Washington, D. C.

Amistad Research Center. American Missionary Association. Archives With References to Schools and Mission Stations. Fisk University, Nashville, Tenn.; microfilm at the University of Maryland at College Park, Maryland.

Barrows, Jasbel, ed. <u>Proceedings of the National Conferenceon Charities and Corrections at the Fifth Annual Session</u>, Boston, Mass.: Geo. H. Ellis, 1878.

Center for American History. Barker History Collection. Minutes of the Cherokee Baptist Association, 1870. University of Texas, Austin.

Minutes of the Presbytery of Eastern Texas, Presbyterian Church in the United States, 1870. Austin, Texas.

Negro Scrapbook. "The Old Time Negroes were imbued with a Spirit Of Loyalty Yet to be Surpassed in These Times—Only a Few Still Live." University of Texas, Austin, Texas.

Pioneer School Records Collection, ca. 1872-1962. University of Texas, Austin, Texas.

Records of Antebellum Southern Plantations from the Revolution Through the Civil War. University of Texas at Austin. Part 1: Texas and Louisiana. Stampp, Kenneth M., ed. Records of Antebellum Southern Plantations from the Revolution through the Civil War.

Series G. Part 1: Texas and Louisiana Collections. microfilm project of University Publications of America, Inc., Frederick, Maryland, 1985.

Works Progress Administration Records—Slave Stories. University of Texas, Austin, Texas.

Christian Methodist Episcopal Church. East Texas Annual Conference Minutes 1912. Jackson, Tenn.: The CME Publishing House, 1912.

Hamilton, Andrew. Governor's Correspondence. Archives,

Texas State Library, Austin.

Harrison County Courthouse. County Clerk Office, Deed Records 1865-1875, Marshall, Texas.

Harrison County Historical Museum. Freedmen's Contracts with Adam Hope File, 1866. Marshall, Texas.

Hill, John. Archives, Texas State Library, Austin, Texas.

Methodist Episcopal Church. Annual Reports of the Freedmen's Aid Society of the Methodist Episcopal Church. Vols. 10-12, 1877-80.

Cincinnati: Western Methodist Book Concern Print, 1878, 1879, 1880.

Powell, Ernest to C. R. Hargrove, M. D., 5 February 1936. File, "Reconstructing Days: Little John, et al." Marshall, Texas.

Texas Department of Health. Bureau of Vital Statistics. Birth and Death Statistics, 1860-1880. Austin, Texas.

Texas Legislature. Resolutions of the State of Texas, Concerning Peace, Reconstruction and Independence. Austin: State Printer, 1865.

Report of the Texas State Lunatic Asylum from October, 1864 to October, 1869. Austin: Tracy, Summering, and Co., 1870.

Texas State Department of Education. Circular and other documents, 1866-1874.

Texas State Library. Davis Papers, 1871. Austin, Texas. Hamilton Papers, 1865. Austin, Texas.

Red River County Court Tax Rolls, 1865-1875. Microfilm Division. Austin, Texas.

Texas Woman's University Special Collections. Ruth Winegarten Collections, Women Studies. Manuscripts on History of Black Women in Texas, Denton, Texas, 1980.

U. S. Adjutant General. Records of the Adjutant General's Office. "Index to the Compiled Service Records of Volunteer Union Soldiers Who Served in Organizations from the State of Texas." Microfilm, Record Group 94. National Archives. Washington, D. C.

U. S. Army, Quartermaster General. <u>Roll of Honor: Names of Soldiers Who Died in Defense of the Union, Interned in the Eastern District of Texas; Central District of Texas; Rio Grande District, Department of Texas; Camp Ford, Tyler, Texas; and Corpus Christi, Texas</u>. Washington, D. C.: Government Printing Office, 1866.

U. S. Bureau of the Census. A Compendium of the Ninth Census, 1870. Washington, D. C.: Government Printing Office, 1872.

U. S. Bureau of the Census. Ninth Census of the United States, 1870: Population. Washington, D. C.: Government Printing Office, 1872.

U. S. Bureau of the Census. Records of the Bureau of the Census. Population Schedule, Ninth Census (1870). Record Group 29. Washington, D. C.

U. S. Bureau of Refugees, Freedmen and Abandoned Lands. Records of the Assistant Commissioner for the State of

Texas, 1865-1869, Roll 1 and Roll 11, Microfilm. National Archives. Washington, D. C.

Letters and Endorsements Sent, Volume 1, No. 5, May—November, 1866-1867, Volume 2, no. 6, April 1869—December 1876. Record Group 105. National Archives. Washington, D. C.

Records of the Superintendent of Education for the State of Texas. Microfilm M-822. National Archives. Washington, D. C.

Register of Letters Received. Texas Records of the Bureau of Refugees, Freedmen, and Abandoned Lands, February 1866-1869. Record Group 105. National Archives. Washington, D. C.

Registered Reports of Operations and Conditions, 1865—1869. Records Group 105. National Archives. Washington, D. C.

U. S. Congress, House of Representatives. Communication from Governor Pease of Texas, Relative to the Troubles in that State. 40th Congress, 2nd session, 1868. H. Misc. Doc. 127.

House Reports. 39th Congress, 1st session, 1866, H. R. 30, 46, 47, 50.

_____. Petitions for Removal of Legal and Political Disabilities Imposed by the 14th Amendment. File 40A-H 21.20. Texas. Record Group 233. National Archives. Washington, D. C.

_____. Report of the Joint Committee in Reconstruction. 39th Congress, 1st sess., 1866. H. Rept. 30.

_____. Select Committee on Reconstruction. "Partition of Texas." File 40A-F 29.36. Record Group 233. National Archives. Washington, D. C.

_____. "Various Texas Affairs." File 40A-F 29.38. Record Group 233. National Archives. Washington, D. C.

_____. "Various Texas Affairs." File 40A-F 29.40. Record Group 233. National Archives. Washington, D. C.

_____. "Various Texas Affairs." File 40A-F 29.41. Record Group 233. National Archives. Washington, D. C.

U. S. Senate. Senate Executive Documents, 39th Congress, 2nd session, 1867, no.6, pp.148-50, Washington, D. C.

Letters of the President of the Constitutional Convention of Texas, 40th Congress, 2nd session, 1868, Miscellaneous Documents, no. 109, pp.3-4, Washington, D. C.

Statutes At Large, 1866. Washington, D. C.: Government Printing Office, 1868.

Newspapers and Magazines

American Missionary X 6 (June, 1866); 10 October 1866.

Austin Democratic Statesman, (Austin, Texas), 3 August, 1871.

Clarksville Standard, (Clarksville, Texas), 5 April, 1869.

East Texas Guard, (Tyler, Texas), 22 July, 1908.

Flake's Bulletin, (Galveston, Texas), 1 January, 1868; 1 April, 1871.

Freeman's Press (also Freedman's Press), (Austin, Texas), 18 July 1868, 25 August 1868.

Galveston Daily News, (Galveston, Texas), 1 October, 12 November, 1865.

Harrison Flag, (Marshall, Texas), 21 September, 1867; 2 May, 1867.

People's Union, (Marshall, Texas), 19 June, 1904.

Southern Intellingencer, 9 November, 1865.

Texas and Louisiana Watchman, (Marshall, Texas), 15 March, 1905.

Texas Republican, (Tyler, Texas), 16 June, 1865.

Unpublished Interviews

Abbott, Lucille. Interview by Author, 28 August 1993, Marshall, Texas, tape recording, Residence, Marshall, Texas.

Chatham, Anis. Interview by Author, 29 August 1993, Tyler, Texas.

East, Bettie. Interview by author, 19 November 1991, 22 August 1992, Cisco, Texas, tape recording, Residence, Cisco, Texas.

Gaines, Arer. Interview by author, 27 August 1993, Marshall, Texas.

Jenkins, Inez. Interview by author, 26 August 1993, Marshall, Texas, tape recording, Residence, Marshall, Texas.

Lee, Leola. Interview by author, 19 November 1991, Cisco, Texas, tape recording, Residence, Cisco, Texas.

Parker, Jennie V. Interview by author, 14 November 1991, 21 August 1992, Ft. Worth, Texas, tape recording, Residence, Cisco, Texas.

Roberson, Lee. Interview by author, 20 November 1991, Cisco, Texas, tape recording, Residence, Cisco, Texas.

Walton, Sue. Interview by Author, 28 August 1993, Tyler, Texas.

Secondary Sources

Abzug, Robert H. "The Black Family During Reconstruction." In Key Issues in the Afro-American Experience, Vol. 2, eds. Nathan Huggins, Martin Kilson, and Daniel Fox, 26-41. New York: Harcourt, Brace, Javonovich, 1971.

Adams, Effie K. Tall Black Texans: Men of Color. Dubuque: Kendall/ Hunt Publishing Co., 1972.

Addington, Wendell G. "Slave Insurrections in Texas." Journal of Negro History 35 (October 1950): 408-34.

Agresti, Barbara F. "The First Decades of Freedom: Black Families in a Southern County, 1870-1885." Journal of Marriage and the Family 40 (November 1978): 697-706.

Alexander, Adele Logan. Ambigious Lives: Free Women of Color In Rural Georgia, 1789-1879. Fayetteville: The University of Arkansas Press, 1991.

Allen, Ruth Alice. The Labor of Women in the Production of Cotton. New York: Arno Press, 1975; originally published, 1931.

Amos, Preston E. Above and Beyond in the West: Black Medal of Honor Winners, 1870-1890. Washington: Potomac Corral, the Westerners, 1974.

Anderson, Eric and Alfred A. Moss, Jr., eds. The Facts of Reconstruction: Essays in Honor of John Hope Franklin. Baton Rouge: Louisiana State University Press, 1991.

Anderson, James D. The Education of Blacks in the South, 1860-1935. Chapel Hill: University of North Carolina Press, 1988.

Anderson, James S. The Sunday School Talker. Austin: Herald Press, 1904.

Aptheker, Bettina. Woman's Legacy: Essays on Race, Sex, and Class in American History. Amherst: University of Massachusetts Press, 1982.

Bardaglio, Peter W. "Challenging Parental Custody Rights: The Legal Reconstruction of Parenthood in the Nineteenth-century American South," Continuity and Change 4 (1989): 259-92.

Barr, Alwyn. Black Leaders: Texans For Their Times. Austin: Texas State Historical Association, 1981.

_____. "Black Legislators of Reconstruction Texas." Civil War History 32 (December 1986): 340-52.

_____. Black Texans: A History of Negroes in Texas, 1528-1971. Austin: Jenkins Publishing Co., 1973.

_____. Reconstruction to Reform Texas Politics, 1876—1906. Austin: University of Texas Press, 1971.

Barrett, Harris (Mrs.). "Negro Women's Clubs and the Community." The Southern Workman 39 (January 1910): 33-34.

Beeth, Howard and Cary D. Wintz, eds. Black Dixie: Afro-Texan History and Culture in Houston. College Station: Texas A & M University Press, 1992.

Bentley, George R. A History of the Freedmen's Bureau. New York: Octagon Books, 1970.

Bercaw, Nancy. "Defeat From Within: Planter Women and the Politics of Household in the Civil War Delta." Southern Historical Association Meeting, November 11, 1993, Orlando, Florida.

Berkeley, Kathleen C. "'Colored Ladies Also Contributed': Black Women's Activities From Benevolence to Social Welfare, 1866-1896." In The Web of Southern Social Relations: Women, Family, and Education, ed. Walter J. Fraser, Jr., R. Frank Saunders,

Jr., and Lon L. Wakelyn, 181-203. Athens: University of Georgia Press, 1985.

Berlin, Ira, et. al., eds. Freedom: A Documentary History of Emancipation: The Wartime Genesis of Free Labor: The Lower South. Cambridge, New York: Cambridge University Press, 1990.

Berlin, Ira, Steven F. Miller, and Leslie S. Rowland. "Afro-American Families in the Transition from Slavery to Freedom." Radical History Review 42 (1988): 89-121.

Bernard, Jesse S. Marriage and Family Among Negroes. New Jersey: Prentice Hall, 1966.

Berry, Mary. "Judging Morality: Sexual Behavior and Legal Consequences in the Late Nineteenth-Century South." The Journal of American History 78, no. 3 (December 1991): 835-56.

Billingsley, Andrew. Black Families In White America. New York: Simon and Schuster, Inc., 1968.

Biola, Heather. "The Black Washer Woman in Southern Tradition." Tennessee Folklore Society Bulletin 45, no. 1 (1979): 17-27.

Blackburn, George and Sherman L. Ricards. "The Mother-Headed Family Among Free Negroes in Charleston, South Carolina, 1850-1860." Phylon 42, no. 1 (Spring 1981): 11-25.

"Black Women as Workers: A Selected Listing of Masters Theses and Doctoral Dissertations." Sage 3 (Spring 1986): 64-66.

Blassingame, John W. Black New Orleans, 1860-1880. Chicago: University of Chicago Press, 1973.

Bleser, Carol, ed. In Joy and Sorrow: Women, Family, and Marriage in the Victorian South, 1830-1900. New York: Oxford University Press, 1991.

Blumenfeld, Emily and Susan Mann. "Domestic Labour and the Reproduction of Labour Power: Towards an Analysis of Women, the Family, and Class." In Hidden in the Household: Women's Domestic Labour under Capitalism, ed. Bonnie Fox, 267-307. Toronto: Women's Press, 1980.

Boatright, Mody C. From Hell to Breakfast. Dallas: Southern Methodist University Press, 1944.

Bogin, Ruth and Bert James Loewenberg, eds. Black Women in Nineteenth Century American Life: Their Words, Their Thoughts, Their Feelings. University Park: Pennsylvania State University Press, 1976.

Boris, Eileen. "Looking At Women's Historians Looking At Difference." Wisconsin Women's Law Journal 3 (1987): 213-38.

Botkin, B. A. Lay My Burden Down: A Folk History of Slavery. Chicago: University of Chicago Press, 1945.

Bracey, John H., Jr. "Afro-American Women: A Brief Guide to Writings from Historical and Feminist Perspectives." Contributions in Black Studies 8 (1986-1987): 106-10.

Brawley, James P. "A Brief Historical Sketch of the Woman's Home Missionary Society; The Methodist Episcopal Church in Relation to The Freeman's Aid Society." Chap. in Two Centuries of Methodist Concern: Bondage, Freedom, and Education of Black People. New York: Vantage Press, 1974.

LaVonne Jackson Leslie, Ph.D.

Brewer, John Mason. <u>Aunt Dicy Tales: Snuff-Dipping Tales of the Texas Negro</u>. Austin: n.p., 1956.

_____. <u>Negro Legislators of Texas and Their Descendants</u>. Dallas: Mathis Publishing Co., 1935.

Brown, Elsa Barkley. "To Catch the Vision of Freedom: Reconstructing Southern Black Women's Political History, 1865-1885." Unpublished paper. (no date).

_____. "Womanist Consciousness: Maggie Lena Walker and the Independent Order of Saint Luke." <u>Signs: Journal of Women in Culture and Society</u> 14 (Spring 1989): 610-33.

Brown, Minnie Miller. "Black Women in Agriculture." <u>Agricultural History</u> 50 (January 1976): 202-12.

Bullock, Henry A. <u>A History of Negro Education in the South: From 1619 to the Present</u>. Cambridge: Harvard University Press, 1967.

Burgess, Norma J., and Hayward Derrick Horton. "African—American Women and Work: A Socio-Historical Perspective." <u>Journal of Family History</u> 18, no. 1 (1993): 53-63.

Burnham, Dorothy. "The Life of the Afro-American Woman in Slavery." <u>International Journal of Women's Studies</u> 1 (July/August 1978): 363-77.

Butchart, Ronald E. <u>Northern Schools, Southern Blacks, and Reconstruction: Freedmen's Education; 1862-1875</u>. Westport: Greenwood Press, 1980.

Bynum, Victoria. "Reshaping the Bonds of Womanhood: Divorce in Reconstruction North Carolina." In <u>Divided Houses: Gender and</u>

the Civil War, ed. Catherine Clinton and Nina Silber, 320-33. New York: Oxford University Press, 1992.

_____. Unruly Women: The Politics of Social and Sexual Control in the Old South. Chapel Hill: University of North CarolinaPress, 1992.

Calvert, Robert A., ed. "The Freedmen and Agricultural Prosperity." Southwestern Historical Quarterly 76 (April 1973): 461-64.

Campbell, Randolph B. An Empire for Slavery: The Peculiar Institution in Texas, 1821-1865. Baton Rouge: Louisiana State University Press, 1989.

_____. "Grass Roots Reconstruction: The Personnel of Country Government in Texas, 1865-1876." The Journal of Southern History 58 (February 1992): 99-116.

_____. "Local Archives as a Source of Slave Prices: Harrison County, Texas." Historian 36 (August 1974): 660-69.

_____. "The Productivity of Slave Labor in East Texas: A Research Note." Louisiana Studies 13 (1974): 154-72.

_____. A Southern Community in Crisis: Harrison County, Texas, 1850-1880. Austin: Texas State Historical Assoc., 1983.

Cantrell, Greg. "Racial Violence & Reconstruction Politics in Texas, 1867-1868." Southwestern Historical Quarterly 93 (January 1990): 333-55.

Carroll, Berenice A., ed. Liberating Women's History: Theoretical and Critical Essays. Urbana: University of Illinois Press, 1976.

Carter, Dan T. When the War Was Over: The Failure of Self-Reconstruction in the South, 1865-1867. Baton Rouge: Louisiana State University Press, 1985.

Casdorph, Paul D. "Some Early Republicans of Smith County, Texas." Chronicles of Smith County, Texas 7 (Fall 1968): 1-6.

Cashin, Herschel V. Under Fire With the Tenth U. S. Cavalry. New York: Bullwalker Pub. Co., 1970.

Christian, Barbara. Black Feminist Criticism: Perspectives on Black Women Writers. New York: Pergamon Press, 1985.

Clark, William T. Children's Rights—Schools for All: Speech of Hon. William T. Clark of Texas, Delivered in the House of Reps, February 8, 1871. Washington: F. & J. Rives and G. A. Bailey, 1871.

Clarke, Robert L., ed. Afro-American History: Sources for Research. Washington, D. C.: Howard University Press, 1981.

Clinton, Catherine. "Bloody Terrain: Freedwomen, Sexuality, and Violence During Reconstruction." The Georgia Historical Quarterly 76 (Summer 1992): 313-32.

_____. "Caught in the Web of the Big House: Women and Slavery." In The Web of Southern Social Relations: Women, Family, and Education, ed. Walter J. Fraser, Jr., R. Frank Saunders, Jr., and Jon L. Wakelyn, 19-34. Athens: University of Georgia Press, 1985.

_____. "Reconstructing Freedwomen." In Divided Houses: Gender and the Civil War, ed. Catherine Clinton and Nina Silber, 306-19. New York: Oxford University Press, 1992.

_____. "Southern Dishonor: Flesh, Blood, Race, and Bondage." In Joy and Sorrow: Women, Family, and Marriage in the Victorian South, 1830-1900, ed. Carol Bleser, 52-68. New York: Oxford University Press, 1991.

Cohen-Lack, "A Struggle for Sovereignty: National Consolidation, Emancipation, and Free Labor in Texas." Journal of Southern History 58 (February 1992): 57-98.

Combahee River Collective. "A Black Feminist Statement." In Capitalist Patriarchy and the Case for Socialist Feminism, ed. Zillah R. Eisenstein, 362-72. New York: Monthly Review Press, 1979.

Cooper, Anna Julia. A Voice from the South: By a Black Woman of the South. 1892; reprint, New York: Negro Universities Press, 1969.

Cott, Nancy. The Bonds of Womanhood: Woman's Sphere in New England, 1700-1835. New Haven, Conn.: Yale University Press, 1977.

_____. The Grounding of Modern Feminism. New Haven: Yale University Press, 1987.

Cotton, Walter F. History of Negroes of Limestone County from 1860 to 1939. Mexia: J. A. Chatman and S. M. Merriwether, 1939.

Cox, LaWanda. "The Promise of Land for the Freedmen." Mississippi Valley Historical Review 45 (December 1958): 413-40.

Crouch, Barry A. "'All the Vile Passions': The Texas Black Code of 1866," Southwestern Historical Quarterly 97 (July 1993): 13-34.

_____. "Black Dreams and White Justice." Prologue 6 (Winter 1974): 255-65.

_____. "The "Chords of Love": Legalizing Black Marital And Family Rights in Postwar Texas." Unpublished manuscript.

_____. The Freedmen's Bureau and Black Texans. Austin: University of Texas Press, 1992.

_____. "The Freedmen's Bureau of the 30th Sub-District in Texas: Smith County and Its Environs during Reconstruction." Chronicles of Smith County, Texas 11 (Spring 1972): 15-30.

_____. "Freedmen's Bureau Records: Texas, A Case Study." In Afro-American History: Sources for Research, ed. Robert L. Clarke, 74-94. Washington, D. C.: Howard University Press, 1981.

_____. "Hesitant Recognition: Texas Black Politicians, 1865-1900." East Texas Historical Journal 31 (1993): 41-58.

_____. "Hidden Sources of Black History: The Texas Freedmen's Bureau Records as a Case Study." Southwestern Historical Quarterly 83 (January 1980): 211-26.

_____. "Seeking Equality: Houston Black Women during Reconstruction." In Black Dixie: Essays on Afro-Texan History in Houston, ed. Howard Beath and Cary Wintz. College Station: Texas A & M University Press, 1992.

_____. "A Spirit of Lawlessness: White Violence, Texas Blacks, 1865-1866." Journal of Social History 18 (Winter 1984): 217-32.

_____. "Unmanacling Texas Reconstruction: A Twenty-Year Perspective." Southwestern Historical Quarterly 93 (January 1990): 275-302.

_____. "View from Within: Letters of Gregory Barrett, Freedmen's Bureau Agent." Chronicles of Smith County, Texas 12 (Winter 1973): 13-26.

Crouch, Barry and Larry Madaras. "Reconstruction Black Families: Perspectives from the Texas Freedmen's Bureau Records." Prologue 18 (Summer 1986): 109-22.

Crouch, Barry A., and L. J. Schultz. "Crisis in Color: Racial Separation in Texas During Reconstruction." Civil War History 16 (March 1969): 37-49.

Croxdale, Richard, and Melissa Hield, eds. Women in the Texas Workforce: Yesterday and Today. Austin: People's History in Texas, 1979.

Crummell, Alexander. "The Black Woman of the South." American Missionary Magazine 42 (April 1888): 105-07.

Cunningham, Constance A. "The Sin of Omission: Black Women In Nineteenth Century American History." Journal of Social and Behavioral Sciences 33, no. 1 (Winter 1987): 35-46.

Dannett, Sylvia G. L., ed. Profiles of Negro Womanhood. Negro Heritage Library. Yonkers: Educational Heritage, 1964.

Davis, Angela Y. "Reflections on the Black Woman's Role in the Community of Slaves." The Black Scholar 3 (December 1971): 3-15.

_____. Women, Race, and Class. New York: Random House, 1981.

Davis, William R. The Development and Present Status of Negro Education in East Texas. New York: Columbia University, 1934; reprint, New York: AMS Press, 1972.

Degener, Edward. The Minority Report in Favor of Extending the Right of Suffrage . . . Made in the Texas Reconstruction Convention, February 24, 1866. Austin: Southern Intelligence Office, 1966.

Degler, Carl. Family Issues At Odds: Women and the Family in America From the Revolution to the Present. New York: Oxford University Press, 1980.

de Graaf, Lawrence B. "Race, Sex, and Region: Black Women in The American West, 1850-1920." Pacific Historical Review 49 (May 1980): 285-313.

Dennett, John Richard. The South As It Is, 1865-1866, ed. Henry M. Christman. New York: Viking Press, 1965.

Dickson, Lynda F. "Toward A Broader Angle of Vision in Uncovering Women's History: Black Women's Clubs Revisited." Frontiers 9, no. 2 (1987): 62-68.

Dill, Bonnie Thornton. "The Dialects of Black Womanhood." Signs: Journal of Women in Culture and Society 4, no. 3 (1979): 543-55.

_____. "'The Means to Put My Children Through': Child Rearing Goals and Strategies Among Black Female Domestic Servants." In The Black Woman, ed. LaFrances Rodgers-Rose, 107-23. Beverly Hills: Sage Publications, Inc., 1980.

_____. "Race, Class, and Gender: Prospects For An All-Inclusive Sisterhood." Feminist Studies 9 (Spring 1983): 131-50.

Dodson, Jualynne. "Nineteenth-Century A. M. E. Preaching Women." In Women in New Worlds, ed. H. F. Thomas and R. S. Keller. Nashville: Abingdon, 1981.

Doss, Harriet E. Amos. "One Aspect of `Domestic Reconstruction`: Women's Missions to Former Slaves in Alabama during Reconstruction." Southern Historical Association Meeting, November 12, 1993, Orlando, Florida.

DuBois, Ellen C. and Vicki L. Ruiz, eds. Unequal Sisters: A Multicultural Reader in U.S. Women's History. New York: Routledge, 1990.

DuBois, William E. B. Black Reconstruction in America: An Essay Toward a History of the Part Which Black Folks Played in the Attempt to Reconstruct Democracy in America, 1860-1880. New York: Atheneum Press, 1979.

_____. Darkwater; rpt. New York: Schocken, 1969.

_____. The Negro American Family. Cambridge: M. I. T. Press, 1909.

_____. What the Negro Has Done for the United States and Texas. Washington, D. C.: U. S. Government Printing Office, 1936.

Dudden, Faye E. Serving Women: Household Service in Nineteenth-Century America. Middletown, Conn.: Wesleyan University Press, 1983.

Dumas, Rhetaugh Graves. "Dilemmas of Black Females in Leadership." In The Black Woman, ed. LaFrances Rodgers-Rose, 203-15. Beverly Hills: Sage Publications, Inc., 1980.

Eaton, John. Grant, Lincoln, and the Freedmen. New York: Longmans, Green, and Co., 1907.

Eblen, Jack E. "New Estimates of the Vital Rates of the United States Black Population During the Nineteenth Century." Demography 11 (May 1974): 301-19.

Eby, Frederick. The Development of Education in Texas. New York: Macmillan Co., 1925.

Edwards, Laura F. "Sexual Violence, Gender, Reconstruction and the Extension of Patriarchy in Granville, North Carolina." North Carolina Historical Review 68 (July 1991): 237-59.

Elliott, Claude. "The Freedman's Bureau in Texas." Southwestern Historical Quarterly 56 (July 1952): 1-24.

Engerman, Stanley L. "Black Fertility and Family Structure in the U.S., 1880-1940." Journal of Family History 1-2 (June 1977): 117-38.

Epstein, Barbara L. The Politics of Domesticity. Middletown: Wesleyan University Press, 1981.

Evans, Sara. Born for Liberty: A History of Women in America. New York: Free Press, 1989.

Exley, Jo Ella. Texas Tears and Texas Sunshine. Voices of Frontier Women. College Station: Texas A & M University Press, 1985.

Farley, Reynolds. Growth of the Black Population: A Study of Demographic Trends. Chicago: Markham Publishing Co., 1970.

Farnham, Christie. "Sapphire? The Issue of Dominance in the Slave Family, 1830-1865." In "To Toil the Livelong Day": America's

Women at Work, 1780-1980, ed. Carol Groneman and Mary Beth Norton, 68-83. Ithaca: Cornell University Press, 1987.

Fine, Betty, et al. Clarksville. Austin: School of Architecture, University of Texas, 1969.

Finkelhor, David. "Common Features of Family Abuse." In Marriage and the Family in a Changing Society, ed. James M. Henslin, 500-07. New York: Free Press, 1985.

Finley, Randy. "Freedperson's Identities and the Freedmen's Bureau in Arkansas, 1865-1869." Southern Historical Association Meeting, November 11, 1993, Orlando, Florida.

Fitzgerald, Michael W. The Union League Movement in the Deep South: Politics and Agricultural Change During Reconstruction. Baton Rouge: Louisiana State University Press, 1989.

Fleming, John E. "Slavery, Civil War and Reconstruction: A Study of Black Women in Microcosms." Negro History Bulletin 38 (August, September 1975): 430-33.

Flexner, Eleanor. A Century of Struggle: The Women's Rights Movement in the United States. Cambridge: Harvard University Press, 1959.

Flynn, Charles L. White Land, Black Labor: Caste and Class in Late Nineteenth Century Georgia. Baton Rouge: Louisiana State University Press, 1983.

Foner, Eric. A Short History of Reconstruction, 1863-1877. New York: Harper and Row, 1990.

_____. Nothin' But Freedom: Emancipation and Its Legacy. Baton Rouge: Louisiana State University Press, 1983.

_____. Reconstruction: America's Unfinished Revolution, 1863-1877. New York: Harper and Row, 1988.

_____. "Rights and the Constitution in Black Life During the Civil War and Reconstruction." Journal of American History 74 (December 1987): 863-83.

Foner, Philip S. Women and the American Labor Movement: From Colonial Times to the Eve of WWI. New York: Macmillan Press, 1979.

Foster, Frances S. "Ultimate Victims: Black Women in Slave Narratives." Journal of American Culture 4 (Winter 1978): 845-63.

Fowler, Arlen L. The Black Infantry in the West, 1869-1891. Westport: Greenwood Publishing Corp., 1971.

Fox-Genovese, Elizabeth. Within the Plantation Household: Black and White Women of the Old South. Chapel Hill: University of North Carolina Press, 1988.

Frankel, Noralee. "Domesticity, Sexuality, Respectability, and the Gendered Vocabulary of Freed Men and Women in Post-bellum Mississippi." Unpublished paper. (no date).

Franklin, John Hope. Reconstruction After the Civil War. Chicago: University of Chicago Press, 1960.

Franklin, John Hope and Alfred A. Moss, Jr. From Slavery to Freedom: A History of Negro Americans, 6th ed. New York: Alfred A. Knopf, 1988.

Fraser, Walter J., R. Frank Saunders Jr., and Jon L. Wakelyn, eds. The Web of Southern Social Relations: Women, Family, and Education. Athens: University of Georgia Press, 1985.

Frazier, Edward Franklin. The Negro Family in the United States. Chicago: University of Chicago Press, 1939.

Friedman, Jean E. "Women's History and the Revision of Southern History." In Sex, Race, and the Role of Women in the South, ed. Joanne V. Hawks and Sheila L. Skemp, 3-12. Jackson: University Press of Mississippi, 1983.

Fuller, Maude Anna, ed. Guide for Woman's Home and Foreign Missionary Societies and Circles. Austin: General Baptist Convention, n.d.

Gatell, Frank Otto and Allen Weinstein, eds. The Segregation Era, 1863-1954, A Modern Reader. New York: Oxford University Press, 1970.

Gammel, Hana Peter Nielson, comp. The Laws of Texas, 1822-1897. Vols. IV-X of 31 vols. Austin: Gammel Book Co., 1898.

Gates, Henry Louis, Jr., ed. Collected Black Women's Narratives. New York: Oxford University Press, 1988.

Gates, Paul W. "Federal Land Policy in the South, 1868-1888." Journal of Southern History 6 (August 1940): 303-30.

Genovese, Eugene D. Roll, Jordan, Roll: The World the Slaves Made. New York: Pantheon Books, 1972.

Gerteis, Louis S. From Contraband to Freedman: Federal Policy Toward Southern Blacks, 1861-1865. Westport, Conn.: Greenwood Publishing Co., 1973.

Giddings, Paula. When and Where I Enter: The Impact of Black Women on Race and Sex in America. New York: William Morrow, 1984.

Gilkes, Cheryl Townsend. "Holding Back The Ocean With A Broom: Black Women and Community Work." In The Black Woman, ed. La Frances Rodgers-Rose, 217-31. Beverly Hills: Sage Publications, Inc., 1980.

_____. "Together and in Harness: Women's Traditions in the Sanctified Church." Signs: Journal of Women in Culture and Society 10 (Summer 1985): 678-99.

Glymph, Thavolia. "Freedpeople and Ex-Masters: Shaping a NewOrder in the Postbellum South, 1865-1868." In Essays on the Postbellum Southern Economy, ed. Thavolia Glymph and John J. Kushma. College Station, Texas: Texas A & M Press for the University of Texas at Arlington, 1985.

_____. "'Ise' Mrs. Tatum Now': Freedom and Black Women's Reconstruction." Southern Historical Association Meeting, November 4-7, 1992, Atlanta, Georgia.

Goldin, Claudia D. "Female Labor Force Participation: The Origin of Black and White Differences, 1870 and 1880." Journal of Economic History 37 (March 1977): 87-112.

Goodson, Martha Graham. "The Slave Narrative Collection: A Tool for Reconstructing Afro-American Women's History." Western Journal of Black Studies 3, no. 26 (1976): 116-22.

Goodwyn, Lawrence C. "Populist Dreams and Negro Rights: East Texas as a Case Study." American Historical Review 76 (December 1971): 1435-56.

Gordon, Linda. "Family Violence, Feminism, and Social Control." Feminist Studies 12 (Summer 1986): 453-79.

Greenwood, Janette Thomas. "'To Exert Our Influence in Every Way Honorable': Black and White Women and Cooperative Social Reform in the Postwar South." Southern Historical Association Meeting, November 12, 1993, Orlando, Florida.

Groneman, Carol and Mary Beth Norton, eds. To Toil the Livelong Day: America's Women at Work, 1780-1980. Ithaca: Cornell University Press, 1987.

Grossberg, Michael. "Who Gets the Child? Custody, Guardianship, and the Rise of A Judicial Patriarchy in Nineteenth-Century America." Feminist Studies 9, no. 2 (Summer 1983): 237-59.

Guest Editorial. "The Impact of Black Women in Education: An Historical Overview." Journal of Negro Education 51, no. 3 (1982): 173-80.

Gutman, Herbert. The Black Family in Slavery and Freedom, 1750-1925. New York: Pantheon Books, 1976.

Hale, Janice. "The Black Woman and Childrearing." In The Black Woman, ed. La Frances Rodgers-Rose, 79-87. Beverly Hills: Sage Publications, Inc., 1980.

Hall, Jacqueline Dowd. Revolt Against Chivalry: Jessie Daniel Ames and the Women's Campaign Against Lynching. New York: Columbia University Press, 1979.

_____. "Women and Lynchings." Southern Exposure 4, no. 4 (Winter 1977): 53-54.

Hare, Maud Cuney (Mrs.). Morris Wright Cuney: A Tribune of the Black People. New York: Crisis Publishers, 1913.

Harley, Sharon. "For the Good of Family and Race: Gender, Work, and Domestic Roles in the Black Community, 1880-1930." Signs: Journal of Culture and Society 15 (Winter 1990): 336-49.

Harley, Sharon and Rosalyn Terborg-Penn. The Afro-American Woman: Struggles and Images. Port Washington, N. Y.: National University Publications, 1978.

_____. "Black Women in a Southern City: Washington, D.C." In Sex, Race, And The Role of Women in the South, ed. Joanne V. Hawks and Sheila L. Skemp, 59-74. Jackson: University Press of Mississippi, 1983.

Harper, Frances Ellen Watkins. "Colored Women of America." Englishwoman's Review 15 (January 1878): 65-68.

Harris, Eula Wallace. Christian Methodist Episcopal Church Through the Years. Jackson, Tenn.: The Methodist Publishing House, 1965.

Hartzell, Joseph. "Methodism and the Negro in the United States." Journal of Negro History 8 (July 1923): 315.

Hays, Roland C. Afro-American Texas Oral History Project. University of Texas at Austin, 1972.

Henderson, Donald H. The Negro Freedman. New York: Cooper Square Publishers, 1971.

Hermann, Janet Sharp. The Pursuit Of A Dream. New York: Oxford University Press, 1981.

Hewitt, Nancy A. "Beyond The Search for Sisterhood: American Women's History in the 1980's." Journal of Social History 10 (October 1985): 1-14.

_____, ed. Women, Families, and Communities: Reading in American History. Glenview: Scott, Foresman, 1990.

Higginbotham, Evelyn Brooks. "African-American Women's History and the Metalanguage of Race." Signs: Journal of Women in Culture and Society 17 (Winter 1992): 251-74.

_____. Beyond the Sound of Silence: Afro-American Women in History." Gender and History 1, no. 1 (Spring 1989): 50-67.

_____. Righteous Discontent: The Women's Movement in the Black Baptist Church, 1880-1920. Boston: Harvard University Press, 1993.

Hine, Darlene Clark, ed. Black Victory: The Rise and Fall of the White Primary in Texas. New York: KTO Press, 1979.

_____. Black Women in America: An Historical Encyclopedia. New York: Carlson Press, 1993.

_____. Black Women in United States History, From Colonial Times to the Present. 16 vols. New York: Carlson Publishing, Inc., 1990.

_____. "Lifting the Veil, Shattering the Silence: Black Women's History in Slavery and Freedom." In The State of Afro-American

History: Past, Present, and Future, ed. Darlene Clark Hine, 223-49. Baton Rouge: Louisiana State University Press, 1986.

_____. The State of Afro-American History: Past, Present, and Future. Baton Rouge: Louisiana State University Press, 1986.

Hobson, Elizabeth. A Report Concerning the Colored Women of the South. Baltimore: J. Murphy & Company, 1896.

Holt, Thomas. Black Over White: Negro Political Leadership in South Carolina During Reconstruction. Urbana: University of Illinois Press, 1977.

Hooks, Bell. Ain't I A Woman: Black Women and Feminism. Boston: South End Press, 1981.

Hornsby, Alton, Jr. "The Freedmen's Bureau Schools in Texas, 1865-1870." Southwestern Historical Quarterly 76 (April 1973): 397-417.

Horton, James O. "Freedom's Yoke: Gender Conventions Among Antebellum Free Blacks." Feminist Studies 12 (Spring 1986): 51-76.

Horton, John. Free People of Color. Washington and London: Smithsonian Institution Press, 1993.

Hull, Gloria T., Patricia Bell Scott, and Barbara Smith. All the Women are White, All the Blacks are Men, But Some of Us are Brave. New York: The Feminist Press, 1982.

Hunt, Annie Mae. I Am Annie Mae. Austin: Rosegarden Press, 1983.

Hunter, Frances L. "Slave Society on the Southern Plantation." Journal of Negro History 7 (January 1922): 1-10.

Hunter, Tera. "The Correct Thing: Charlotte Hawkins Brown And the Palmer Institute." Southern Exposure 11 (Sept./Oct. 1983): 37-43.

_____. "Work, Home, and Leisure: Waged Household Workers, Working-Class Consciousness, and Their Place in the New South." Southern Historical Association Meeting, November 12, 1993, Orlando, Florida.

Institute of Texan Cultures. The Afro-American Texans. San Antonio: The Institute, 1975.

Jamison, M. F. Autobiography and Work of Bishop M. F. Jamison. Nashville: Publishing House of the M. E. Church, South, 1912.

Janiewski, Dolores E. Sisterhood Denied: Race, Gender, and Class in a New South Community. Philadelphia: Temple University Press, 1985.

_____. "Sisters Under Their Skins: Southern Working Women, 1880-1950." In Sex, Race, and the Role of Women in The South, ed. Joanne V. Hawks and Sheila L. Skemp, 13-35. Jackson: University Press of Mississippi, 1983.

Jaynes, Gerald David. Branches Without Roots: Genesis of the Black Working Class in the American South, 1862-1882. New York: Oxford University Press, 1986.

Jennings, Thelma. "'Us Colored Women Had to Go Through a Plenty': Sexual Exploitation of African-American Slave Women." Journal of Women's History 1 (Winter 1990): 45-74.

Jensen, Joan. With These Hands: Women Working on the Land. Old Westbury, N. Y.: Feminist Press, 1981.

Johanssen, Sheila Ryan. "'Herstory' as History: A New Field of Another Fad? In Liberating Women's History: Theoretical and Critical Essays, ed. Bernice A. Carroll, 400-30. Urbana-Champaign: University of Illinois Press, 1976.

Jones, Jacqueline. Labor of Love, Labor of Sorrow: Black Women, Work, and the Family from Slavery to the Present. New York: Basic Books Inc., 1985.

_____. "'My Mother Was Much of a Woman': Black Women, Work, and the Family Under Slavery." Feminist Studies 8 (Summer 1982): 235-70.

_____. "The Political Economy of Sharecropping Families: Blacks and Poor Whites in the Rural South, 1865-1915." In Joy and Sorrow: Women, Family, and Marriage in the Victorian South, 1830-1900. ed. Carol Bleser, 196-214. New York: Oxford University Press, 1991.

_____. Soldiers of Light and Love: Northern Teachers and Georgia Blacks, 1865-1873. Chapel Hill: University of North Carolina Press, 1980.

Jordan, Winthrop D. White Over Black: American Attitudes Toward the Negro, 1550-1812. Chapel Hill: University of North Carolina Press, 1968.

Katz, Maude White. "The Negro Woman and the Law." Freedomways (Summer 1962): 278-86.

_____. "She Who Would Be Free, Resistance. The Negro Woman in Slavery, in the Civil War and Reconstruction. Freedomways 2 (Winter 1962): 60-70.

Kealing, H. T. History of African Methodism in Texas. Waco: C. F. Blanks, 1885.

Kelly, Joan. Women, History, and Theory: The Essays of Joan Kelly. Chicago: University of Chicago Press, 1984.

Kessler-Harris, Alice. Out to Work: A History of Wage-Earning Women in the United States. New York: Oxford University Press, 1982.

King, Deborah K. "Multiple Jeopardy, Multiple Consciousness: The Context of A Black Feminist Ideology." Signs: Journal Of Women in Culture and Society 14, no. 1 (1988): 42-72.

King, Edward. Texas: 1874; An Eyewitness Account of Conditions in Post-Reconstruction Texas. Houston: Cordoran Press, 1974.

Kirchberger, Joe H. The Civil War and Reconstruction: An Eyewitness Account. New York: Facts on File, 1991.

Kolchin, Peter. First Freedom: The Responses of Alabama's Blacks to Emancipation and Reconstruction. Westport, Conn.: Greenwood Press, 1972.

Krech, Shepard, III. "Black Family Organization in the Nineteenth Century: An Ethnological Perspective." Journal of Interdisciplinary History 12 (Winter 1982): 429-52.

Kugler, Israel. From Ladies to Women: The Organized Struggle For Woman's Rights in the Reconstruction Era. Westport, Conn.: Greenwood Press, Inc., 1987.

Ladner, Joyce A. "Racism and Tradition: Black Womanhood in Historical Perspective." In The Black Woman Cross-Culturally, ed. Filomina Steady, 269-88. Cambridge: Scheckman Publishing, 1981.

_____. Tomorrows' Tomorrow: The Black Woman. Garden City: Doubleday Press, 1971.

Lantz, Herman and Lewellyn Hendrix. "Black Fertility and the Black Family in the 19th Century: A Re-Examination of the Past." Journal of Family History 3 (Fall 1978): 251-61.

Lebsock, Suzanne. The Free Women of Petersburg: Status and Culture in a Southern Town, 1784-1860. New York: W. W. Norton, 1984.

_____. "Radical Reconstruction and the Property Rights of Southern Women." Journal of Southern History 42 (May 1977): 195-216.

Ledbetter, Billy D. "White Texan's Attitudes Towards the Political Equality of Negroes, 1865-1870." Phylon 40, no. 3 (September 1979): 253—.

Lentz, Sallie M. "Highlights of Early Harrison County." Southwestern Historical Quarterly 61 (October 1957): 240-56.

Lerner, Gerda, ed. Black Women in White America: A Documentary History. New York: Random House Inc., 1972.

_____. The Creation of Patriarchy. New York: Oxford University Press, 1986.

_____. "Early Community Work of Black Club Women." Journal of Negro History 59 (April 1974): 158-67.

_____. The Female Experience: An American Documentary. Indianapolis: Bobbs-Merrill Educational Publishers, 1977.

_____. The Majority Finds Its Past. New York: Oxford University Press, 1979.

_____. "New Approaches To the Study of Women in American History." In Liberating Women's History:

Theoretical and Critical Essays, ed. Bernice A. Carroll, 357-68. Urbana-Champaign: University of Illinois Press, 1976.

_____. "Placing Women in History: A 1975 Perspective." In Liberating Women's History: Theoretical and Critical Essays, ed. Bernice A. Carroll, 349-56. Urbana-Champaign: University of Illinois Press, 1976.

Levin, J. S. "The Role of the Black Church in Community Medicine." Journal of the National Medical Association 76 (May 1984): 477-83.

Levine, Lawrence W. Black Culture and Black Consciousness: Afro-American Folk Thought from Slavery to Freedom. Oxford: Oxford University Press, 1977.

Lewis, Diane K. "A Response to Inequality: Black Women, Racism, and Sexism." Signs: Journal of Women in Culture and Society 3 (Winter 1977): 339-61.

Litwack, Leon F. Been in the Storm So Long. New York: Alfred A. Knopf, 1979.

Loewenberg, Bert J. & Ruth Bogin, eds. Black Women in Nineteenth Century American Life: Their Words, Their Thoughts, Their Feelings. University Park: Pennsylvania State University Press, 1976.

Lorde, Audre. "Scratching the Surface: Some Notes On Barriers to Women and Loving." The Black Scholar (April 1978) 31-35.

Malson, Micheline R., ed., et al. Black Women in America: Social Science Perspective. Chicago: University of Chicago Press, 1990.

Mann, Susan A. "Sharecropping in the Cotton South: A Case of Uneven Capitalist Development in Agriculture." Rural Sociology 39 (1984): 412-29.

_____. "Slavery, Sharecropping, and Sexual Inequality." Signs: Journal of Women in Culture And Society 14 (Summer 1989): 774-98.

Marable, Manning. "Grounding With My Sisters: Patriarchy and the Exploitation of Black Women." The Journal of Ethnic Studies 11 (Summer 1983): 1-39.

Marten, James. Texas Divided: Loyalty and Dissent in the Lone Star State, 1856-1874. Lexington: The University Press of Kentucky, 1990.

Martin, Elmer P. and Joanne Mitchell Martin. "The Black Woman: Perspectives on Her Role in the Family." In Ethnicity and Women, ed. Winston A. Van Horne, 184-205. Madison: University of Wisconsin Press, 1986.

Mathis, Pat B. Clark. The History of Clarksville and Old Red River County. Dallas: Van Nort and Co., 1937.

May, Elaine Tyler. "Expanding the Past: Recent Scholarship on Women in Politics and Work." Reviews in American History 10 (December 1982): 216-33.

May, J. T. "A Nineteenth-Century Medical Care Program for Blacks: The Case of Freedmen's Bureau." Anthropological Papers of the University of Alaska 46 (July 1973): 160-71.

McAdoo, Harriet Pipes. Black Families, 2nd ed. Newbury Park, Calif.: Sage Publications, 1988.

_____. "Black Mothers and the Extended Family Support Network." In The Black Woman, ed. La Frances Rodgers-Rose, 125-44. Beverly Hills: Sage Publications, Inc., 1980.

McCray, Carrie Allen. "The Black Woman and Family Roles." In The Black Woman, ed. La Frances Rodgers-Rose, 67-78. Beverly Hills: Sage Publications, Inc., 1980.

McDowell, John Patrick. The Social Gospel in the South: The Woman's Home Mission Movement in the Methodist Episcopal Church, South, 1886-1939. Baton Rouge: Louisiana State University Press, 1982.

McFeely, William S. Yankee Stepfather: General O. O. Howard And the Freedmen. New Haven: Yale University Press, 1978.

McLaurin, Melton A. Celia, A Slave. A True Story of Violence and Retribution in Antebellum Missouri. Athens: University of Georgia Press, 1991.

McMillen, Sally G. Motherhood in the Old South: Pregnancy, Childbirth, and Infant Rearing. Baton Rouge: Louisiana State University Press, 1990.

_____. "Goals and Successes of Southern Black Sunday School Movement, 1865-1915." Southern Historical Association Meeting, November 12, 1993, Orlando, Florida.

Meeker, Edward. "Mortality Trends of Southern Blacks, 1850-1910: Some Preliminary Findings." Explanations in Economic History 13 (January 1976): 13-42.

Meier, August. "Negroes in the First and Second Reconstructions of the South." Civil War History 13 (June 1967): 114-30.

Mohr, James C. Abortion in America: The Origins and Evolution of National Policy. New York: Oxford University Press, 1978.

Moneyhon, Carl H. "Public Education and Texas Reconstruction Politics, 1871-1874." Southwestern Historical Quarterly 92 (January 1989): 393-416.

Montgomery, William E. Under Their Own Vine and Fig Tree: The African-American Church in the South, 1865-1900. Baton Rouge: Louisiana University Press, 1992.

Morris, Robert C. Reading, Riting, and Reconstruction: The Education of Freedmen in the South, 1861-1870. Chicago: University of Chicago Press, 1981.

Morton, Patricia. Disfigured Images: The Historical Assault on Afro-American Women. New York: Greenwood Press, 1991.

Mossell, N. F. The Work of the Afro-American Woman. Philadelphia: G. S. Ferguson, 1894.

Muir, Andrew F. "The Free Negro in Jefferson and Orange Counties, Texas." Journal of Negro History 35 (April 1950): 183—.

Neal, Diane and Thomas W. Kremm. "'What Shall We Do With the Negro?': The Freedmen's Bureau in Texas." East Texas Historical Journal 27 (1989): 23-34.

Neverdon-Morton, Cynthia. Afro-American Women of the South And the Advancement of the Race, 1895-1925. Knoxville: The University of Tennessee Press, 1989.

_____. "Self-Help Programs as Educative Activities of Black Women in the South, 1895-1925: Focus on Four Key Areas." Journal of Negro Education 51 (September 1982): 207-21.

_____. "Through the Looking Glass: Reviewing Books About The Afro-American Female Experience." Feminist Studies 14 (Fall 1988): 612-17.

Newman, Debra L. Black History: A Guide to Civilian Records in the National Archives. Washington, D. C.: National Archives Trust Fund Board, 1984.

_____. Guide to Reconstruction History Sources at the Library of Congress. Washington, D. C.: Library of Congress, 1992.

Nieman, Donald G. To Set the Law in Motion: The Freedmen's Bureau and the Legal Rights of Blacks, 1865-1868. Mellwood, N. Y.: KTO Press, 1979.

Noble, Jeanne. Beautiful Also Are the Souls of My Black Sisters: A History of the Black Woman in America. Englewood Cliffs: Prentice-Hall Inc., 1978.

Norvell, James K. "The Reconstruction Courts of Texas, 1867-1873." Southwestern Historical Quarterly Review, vol. 62, no. 2 (October 1958):.

Olmsted, Frederick Law. <u>The Cotton Kingdom</u>. Edited by Arthur M. Schlesinger. New York: Random House, 1969.

_____. <u>A Journey Through Texas: A Saddle-Trip on the Southwestern Frontier</u>. New York: Mason Brothers, 1860.

Oubre, Claude F. <u>Forty Acres and a Mule: The Freedmen's Bureau and Black Land Ownership</u>. Baton Rouge: Louisiana State University Press, 1978.

Owens, Leslie Howard. <u>This Species of Property: Slave Life and Culture in the Old South</u>. New York: Oxford University Press, 1976.

Painter, Nell Irvin. "Introduction: The Journal of Ella Gertrude Clanton Thomas: An Educated White Woman in the Eras of Slavery, War, and Reconstruction." In <u>The Secret Eye: The Journal of Ella Gertrude Clanton Thomas, 1848-1889</u>, ed. Virginia Ingraham Burr, 1-67. Chapel Hill: University of North Carolina Press, 1990.

_____. "Social Equality, Miscegenation, Labor, and Power." Papers originally delivered at a symposium held at the University of Georgia in October, 1985. In <u>The Evolution of Southern Culture</u>, ed. Numan V. Bartley, 47-67. Athens: University of Georgia Press, 1988.

Palmer, Phyllis M. "White Women/Black Women: The Dualism of Female Identity and Experience in the United States." <u>Feminist Studies</u> 9 (Spring 1983):.

Pemberton, Doris H. <u>Juneteenth at Comanche Crossing</u>. Austin: Eakin Publishing, 1983.

Phillips, C. H. The History of the Colored Methodist Episcopal Church in America. Jackson, Tenn.: The CME Publishing House, 1923.

Pitre, Merline. Through Many Dangers, Toils, and Snares: The Black Leadership of Texas, 1868-1900. Austin: Eakin Press, 1985.

Pleck, Elizabeth. "Wife Beating in Nineteenth-Century America." Victimology 4 (1979): 60-74.

Pogrebin, Letty Cottin. Family Politics: Love and Power on an Intimate Frontier. New York: McGraw-Hill, 1984.

Powell, Lawrence N. New Masters: Northern Planters During the Civil War and Reconstruction. New Haven: Yale University Press, 1980.

Prestage, Jewel L. "Political Behavior of American Blackwomen: An Overview." In The Black Woman, ed. La Frances Rodgers-Rose, 233-49. Beverly Hills: Sage Publications, Inc., 1980.

Rable, George C. But There Was No Peace: The Role of Violence in the Politics of Reconstruction. Athens: University of Georgia Press, 1984.

Ramsdell, Charles W. Reconstruction in Texas. New York: Longmans, Green and Co., 1910.

Ransom, Roger and Richard Sutch. One Kind of Freedom: The Economic Consequences of Emancipation. New York: Cambridge University Press, 1977.

Rapport, Sara. "The Freedmen's Bureau as a Legal Agent for Black Men and Women in Georgia: 1865-1868." Georgia Historical Quarterly 73 (Spring 1989): 39-41.

Rawick, George P., ed. The American Slave: A Composite Autobiography. Vol. 4. Texas Narratives, Parts 1 and 2. Westport: Greenwood Publishing Co., 1972.

_____. The American Slave: A Composite Autobiography. Vol. 5. Texas Narratives, Parts 3 and 4. Westport: Greenwood Publishing Co., 1972.

_____. The American Slave: A Composite Autobiography. Supplement Series 2. Vol. 6. Texas Narratives, Part 5. Westport: Greenwood Publishing Co., 1972.

Redwine, W. A. Brief History of the Negro in Five Counties. Tyler, Texas: n.p., 1901; reprint, Chronicles of Smith County, Texas 11 (Fall 1972): 14-99.

Rice, Lawrence. The Negro in Texas, 1874-1900. Baton Rouge: Louisiana State University Press, 1971.

Rice, Mitchell F. and Woodrow Jones, Jr. Black American Health: An Annotated Bibliography. Westport, Conn.: Greenwood Press, Inc., 1987.

_____. Health of Black Americans from Post-Reconstruction to Integration, 1871-1960: An Annotated Bibliography of Contemporary Sources. Westport, Conn.: Greenwood Press, Inc., 1990.

Richardson, Joe M. Christian Reconstruction: The American Missionary Association and Southern Blacks, 1861-1890. London; Athens: University of Georgia Press, 1986.

Richter, "The Army and the Negro during Texas Reconstruction, 1865-1870." East Texas Historical Journal 10 (Spring 1972): 7-19.

Richter, William L. Overreached on All Sides: The Freedmen's Bureau Administration in Texas, 1865-1868. College Station: Texas A & M University Press, 1991.

_____. "'The Revolver Rules the Day!' Colonel DeWitt C. Brown & the Freedmen's Bureau in Paris, Texas, 1867-1868." Southwestern Historical Quarterly 93 (January 1990): 303-32.

Riley, Glenda. Inventing the American Woman: A Perspective On Women's History. Arlington Heights, Ill.: Harlan Davidson, Inc., 1986.

Rodgers-Rose, La Frances, ed. The Black Woman. Beverly Hills: Sage Publications, 1980.

Rodnitzky, Shirley, ed. A Calendar of the Gaffney Family Papers, 1840-1915. Arlington: The University of Texas at Arlington Press, 1986.

Rose, Willie Lee. Rehearsal For Reconstruction: The Port Royal Experiment. Indianapolis: Bobbs-Merrill, 1964.

Rothman, Ellen K. Hands and Hearts: A History of Courtship in America. New York: Basic Books, Inc., 1984.

Rouse, Jacqueline Anne. Lugenia Burns Hope: Black Southern Reformer. Athens: University of Georgia Press, 1989.

Ryan, Mary P. "The Power of Women's Networks: A Case Study of Female Moral Reform in Antebellum America." Feminist Studies 5 (Spring 1979): 66-86.

_____. Women in Public: Between Banners and Ballots, 1825-1880. Baltimore, Md.: Johns Hopkins University Press, 1990.

Sachs, Carolyn E. The Invisible Farmers: Women in Agricultural Production. Totowa, N.J.: Rowman and Allanheld, 1983.

Salem, Dorothy. To Better Our World: Black Women in Organized Reform, 1890-1920. Brooklyn: Carlson Publishing, 1990.

Schipper, Martin. A Guide to Records of Antebellum Southern Plantations from the Revolution through the Civil War. Series G, Part 1. Frederick, Md.: University Publications of America, Inc., 1985.

Schwalm, Leslie A. "In Their Own Way And At Such Times As They Think Fit: Work and Family in Former Slave Women's Definition of Freedom, 1865-1867." Paper Presented at the Annual Meeting of the Southern Historical Association, November 4-7, 1992, Atlanta, Georgia.

Schweninger, Loren. Black Property Owners in the South, 1790-1915. Urbana and Chicago: University of Illinois Press, 1990.

_____. "Property Owning Free African-American Women in the South, 1800-1870." Journal of Women's History 1 (Winter 1990): 13-44.

Scott, Anne Firor. "Historians Construct the Southern Woman." In Sex, Race, and the Role of Women in the South, ed. Joanne V. Hawks and Sheila L. Skemp, 95-110. Jackson: University Press of Mississippi, 1983.

_____. "Most Invisible of All: Black Women's Voluntary Associations." Journal of Southern History 56 (February 1990): 3-22.

_____. The Southern Lady: From Pedestal to Politics, 1830-1930. Chicago: University of Chicago Press, 1970.

Scott, Joan W. "Gender: A Useful Category of Historical Analysis." American Historical Review 91, no. 5 (December 1986): 1053-75.

Scott, Rebecca J. "The Battle Over the Child: Child Apprenticeship and the Freedmen's Bureau in North Carolina," Prologue 10 (Summer 1978): 101-13.

Shapiro, Herbert. White Violence and Black Response: From Reconstruction to Montgomery. Amherst: University of Massachusetts Press, 1988.

Shockley, Ann Allen. Afro-American Women Writers, 1746-1933: An Anthology and Critical Guide. New York: New American Library, 1989.

Sides, Sudie Duncan. "Southern Women and Slavery." History Today 20 (January 1970): 54-50.

Silverthorne, Elizabeth. Plantation Life in Texas. College Station: Texas A & M University Press, 1986.

Sims, Janet L., comp. The Progress of Afro-American Women: A Selected Bibliography and Resource Guide. Westport, Conn.: Greenwood Press, 1980.

Singletary, Otis A. Negro Militia and Reconstruction. Austin: University of Texas Press, 1957.

Smallwood, James W. "Black Education in Reconstruction Texas: The Contributions of the Freedmen's Bureau and Benevolent Societies," East Texas Historical Journal 19 (January 1981) 17-40.

_____. "Black Texans During Reconstruction: First Freedom." East Texas Historical Journal 14 (Spring 1976): 9-23.

_____. "Emancipation and the Black Family: A Case Study in Texas." Social Science Quarterly 47 (March 1977): 849-57.

_____. "Perpetuation of Caste: Black Agricultural Workers in Reconstruction Texas." MidAmerica 61 (January 1979): 5-23.

_____. Time of Hope, Time of Despair: Black Texans During Reconstruction. Port Washington, N. Y.: Kennikat Press, 1981.

_____. "When the Klan Rode: White Terror in Reconstruction Texas." Journal of the West 25 (October 1986): 4-13.

Smith-Rosenberg, Carroll. "Beauty, the Beast, and the Militant Woman: A Case Study in Sex Roles and Social Stress in Jacksonian America." In A Heritage of Her Own, ed. Nancy F. Cott and Elizabeth H. Pleck, 197-221. New York: Simon and Schuster, 1979.

_____. "The Female World of Love and Ritual: Relations Between Women in Nineteenth-Century America."; reprinted in Cott & Pleck, eds., Heritage and Gordon, ed., American Family, 2nd and 3rd editions.

Smyrl, Frank H. "Texans in the Federal Army, 1861-1865." Southwestern Historical Quarterly 65 (October 1961): 234-50.

Sneed, Edgar P. "A Historiography of Reconstruction in Texas: Some Myths and Problems." Southwestern Historical Quarterly 72 (April 1969): 435-48.

Sparks, Randy J. "'To Move A World': Race, Gender and Modernization in Mississippi Evangelical Churches, 1830-1860." Southern

Historical Association Meeting, November 12, 1993, Orlando, Florida.

Stack, Carol B. All Our Kin: Strategies for Survival in a Black Community. New York: Harper and Row, 1974.

Staples, Robert. The Black Woman in America: Sex, Marriage, and the Family. Chicago: Nelson Hall Publishers, 1978.

Steady, Filomina C., ed. The Black Woman Cross-Culturally. Cambridge: Schenkman Publishing Co., 1981.

Steckel, Richard H. "Slave Marriage and the Family." Journal of Family History 5 (1980): 406-21.

Sterling, Dorothy, ed. The Trouble They Seen: Black People Tell the Story of Reconstruction. Garden City, N. Y.: Doubleday, 1976.

_____. We Are Your Sisters: Black Women in the Nineteenth Century. New York: W. W. Norton, 1984.

Suggs, Henry Lewis, ed. The Black Press in The South, 1865-1979. Westport, Conn.: Greenwood Press, 1983.

Swerdlow, Amy and Hanna Lessinger, eds. Class, Race, and Sex: The Dynamics of Control. Boston: G. K. Hall, 1983.

Swint, Henry Lee. The Northern Teacher in the South, 1862-1870. New York: Octagon Books, 1967.

Tatum, Charles Edward. Mount Zion: In the Shadow of a Mighty Rock, Centennial Edition, 1877-1977. Houston: C. Edwards and Associates, 1977.

Tatum, Charles E. and Lawrence M. Sommers. "The Spread of the Black Christian Methodist Episcopal in the United States, 1870 to 1970." Journal of Geography 74 (September 1975): 343-57.

Taylor, Arnold H. Travail and Triumph. Black Life and Culture in the South Since the Civil War. Westport, Conn.: Greenwood Press, 1976.

Terborg-Penn, Rosalyn. "Discrimination Against Afro—American Women in the Women's Movement, 1830-1920." In The Afro-American Woman: Struggles and Images. Rosalyn Terborg-Penn and Sharon Harley, eds., 17-27. Port Washington: Kennikat Press, 1978.

Terrell, Mary Church. "The Club Work of Colored Women." The Southern Workman 30 (1901): 435-38.

_____. "The History of the Club Women's Movement." The Aframerican Woman's Journal 1 (Summer/Fall 1940): 34-38.

The Texas Almanac for 1868, with Federal and State Statistics, Historical Descriptive, and Biographical Sketches, Etc.,Relating to Texas. Galveston: W. Richardson and Co., 1867.

Texas Teachers' State Association. Proceedings of the Texas Teachers' State Convention . . . 1866. Louisville: John P. Morton & Co., 1866.

Trelease, Allen W. White Terror: The Ku Klux Klan Conspiracy and Southern Reconstruction. New York: Harper and Row, 1971.

Tyler, Ronnie C. and Lawrence R. Murphy. The Slave Narratives of Texas. Austin: The Encino Press, 1974.

University of Texas Institute of Texan Cultures at San Antonio. The Afro-American Texans. San Antonio: The Institute, 1975.

Van Horne, Winston A., ed. Ethnicity and Women. Milwaukee: University of Wisconsin System, American Ethnic Studies Coordinating Committee, Urban Corridor Consortium, 1986.

Vaughn, William. Schools For All: The Blacks and Public Education in the South, 1865-1877. Lexington: University Press of Kentucky, 1974.

Vlach, John. By the Work of Their Hands: Studies in Afro-American Folklife. Ann Arbor: UMI Research Press, 1992.

Walker, Clarence E. A Rock In a Weary Land: The African Methodist Episcopal Church During the Civil War And Reconstruction. Baton Rouge: Louisiana State University Press, 1982.

Wallace, Ernest. The Howling of the Coyotes. College Station: Texas A & M University Press, 1979.

Wallace, Phyllis Ann. Black Women in the Labor Force. Cambridge: M. I. T. Press, 1980.

Washington, Booker T. (Mrs.). "Social Improvement of the Plantation Woman." Voice of the Negro 1 (July 1904): 288-90.

Washington, Margaret Murray. "Club Work Among Negro Women." In The New Progress of a Race, eds. J. L. Nichols and William H. Crogman, 177-209. Naperville: J. L. Nichols & Company, 1929.

Washington, Mary Helen. Invented Lives: Narratives of Black Women 1860-1960. New York: Doubleday, 1987.

Wesley, Charles H. The History of the National Association Of Colored Women's Clubs: A Legacy of Service. rpt. Washington, D. C.: The Association, 1984.

_____. Negro Labor in the United States, 1850-1925. New York: Vanguard Press Inc., 1927.

White, Deborah Gray. Arn't I A Woman? Female Slaves in the Plantation South. New York and London: W. W. Norton and Co., 1985.

_____. "Female Slaves: Sex Roles and Status in the Antebellum Plantation South." Journal of Family History 8, no. 3 (Fall 1983): 248-61.

Williams, David A. Bricks Without Straw: A History of Higher Education for Black Texans, 1872-1971. Austin: D. A. Williams, 1980.

_____. The Emancipation Proclamation of 1863 and the Emancipation Proclamation, Texas Style (June 19, 1865). Austin: Williams Independent Research Enterprises, 1979.

Williams, Fannie B. "The Club Movement Among Colored Women of America." In A New Negro for a New Century, Booker T. Washington, 378-405. Chicago: American Publishing House, 1900.

_____. "Club Movement Among Negro Women." In Progress of a Race, eds. J. L. Nichols and William H. Crogman, 197-231. Naperville: J. L. Nichols & Company, 1929.

Williams, Sylvania F. "The Social Status of the Negro Woman." Voice of the Negro 1 (July 1904): 298-300.

Wilson, Geraldine L. "The Self/Group Actualization of Black Women." In The Black Woman, ed. La Frances Rodgers-Rose, 301-14. Beverly Hills: Sage Publications, 1980.

Winegarten, Ruthe. Finder's Guide to the Texas Woman: A Celebration of History Exhibit Archives. Denton: Texas Woman's University Library, 1984.

_____. "I Am Annie Mae: The Personal Story of a Texas Black Woman." Chrysalis (Spring 1980): 14-23.

Woloch, Nancy. Women and the American Experience. New York: Knopf, 1984.

Wood, Peter H. Winslow Homer's Images of Blacks: The Civil War and Reconstruction Years. Austin: University of Texas Press, 1988.

Woodson, Carter G. The Negro Wage Earner. New York: Van Rees Press, 1930.

_____. The Rural Negro. rpt., New York: Russell and Russell, 1969.

Woodward, C. Vann. Thinking Back: The Perils of Writing History. Baton Rouge: Louisiana State University Press, 1986.

Yearwood, Lennox S., ed. Black Organizations: Issues on Survival Techniques. Lanham, Md.: Institute for Urban Affairs and Research, University Press of America, Inc., 1980.

Dissertations and Theses

Adams, Larry Earl. "Economic Development in Texas During Reconstruction." Ph.D. diss., University of North Texas, 1980.

Bardaglio, Peter. "Families, Sex, and the Law: The Legal Transformation of the Nineteenth Century Southern Household." Ph.D. diss., Stanford University, 1987.

Bartha, Shell, Jr. "A History of the Negro Presbyterian Church U. S. in Texas." Thesis, Univ. of Texas at Austin, 1965.

Berkeley, Kathleen C. "Like A Plague of Locust: Immigration and Social Change in Memphis, Tennessee, 1850-1880." Ph.D. diss., University of California—Los Angeles, 1980.

Brooks, Evelyn. "The Women's Movement in the Black Baptist Church, 1880-1920." Ph.D. diss., University of Rochester, 1984.

Christopher, Nehemiah M. "The History of Negro Public Education in Texas, 1865-1900." Ph.D. diss., University of Pittsburgh, 1948.

Chunn, Prentis W., Jr. "Education and Politics, A Study of the Negro in Reconstruction Texas." Thesis, Southwest Texas State College, 1957.

Colby, Ira Christopher. "The Freedmen's Bureau in Texas and Its Impact on the Emerging Social Welfare System and Black-White Social Relations, 1865-1885." Ph.D. diss., University of Pennsylvania, 1984.

Coleman, Willie Mae. "Keeping the Faith and Disturbing the Peace. Black Women From Anti-Slavery to Women's Suffrage." Ph.D. diss., University of California, Irvine, 1982.

Curlee, Abigail. "A Study of Texas Slave Plantations, 1822 to 1865." Master's Thesis, University of Texas, 1932.

David, Hilda B. "The African-American Women of the Edisto Island: 1850-1920." Ph.D. diss., Emory University, 1990.

Dorsett, Jesse. "Blacks In Reconstruction Texas, 1865-1877." Ph.D. diss., Texas Christian University, 1981.

Dudney, Ross Nathaniel, Jr. "Texas Reconstruction: The Role of the Bureau of Refugees, Freedmen, and Abandoned Lands,1865-1870, Smith County (Tyler), Texas." M.A. thesis, Texas A & I University, 1986.

Edwards, John A. "Social and Cultural Activities of Texans During Civil War and Reconstruction, 1861-1873." Ph.D. diss., Texas Tech University, 1985.

Edwards, Laura F. "The Politics of Manhood and Womanhood: Reconstruction in Granville County, North Carolina." Ph.D. diss., University of North Carolina at Chapel Hill, 1991.

Fields, Emma. "The Women's Club Movement in the United States, 1877-1900." Master's thesis, Howard University, 1948.

Frankel, Noralee. "Workers, Wives, and Mothers: Black Women in Mississippi, 1860-1870." Ph.D. diss., George Washington University, 1983.

Graham, Mary-Emma. "The Threefold Cord: Blackness, Womanness and Art: A Study of the Life and Work of Frances Ellen Watkins." Master's thesis, Cornell University, Ithaca, New York, 1973.

Grobe, Charles William. "Black Newspapers in Texas, 1866-1970." Ph.D. diss., University of Texas at Austin, 1972.

Guy-Sheftall, Beverly. "Daughters of Sorrow: Attitudes Toward Black Women: 1880-1920." Ph.D. diss., Emory University, 1984.

Hill, John Thomas. "The Negro in Texas During Reconstruction." Master's thesis, Texas Christian University, 1965.

Hodes, Martha E. "Sex Across the Color Line: White Women and Black Men in the Nineteenth Century American South." Ph.D. diss., Princeton University, 1991.

Hunter, Tera W. "Household Workers in the Making: Afro-American Women in Atlanta in the New South, 1861-1920." Ph.D. diss., Yale University, 1990.

Kinsey, Winston L. "Negro Labor in Texas, 1865-1876." Master's thesis, Baylor University, 1965.

Kirven, Lamar L. "A Century of Warfare: Black Texans." Ph.D. diss., Indiana University, 1974.

Lavender, Mary Alice. "Social Conditions in Houston and Harris County, 1869-1872." Master's thesis, Rice Institute, 1950.

Mack-Williams, Voloria C. "Hard-Working Women: Class Divisions and African-American Women's Work in Orangeburg, South Carolina, 1880-1940." Ph.D. diss., State University of New York at Binghampton, 1991.

Montgomery, Carol Lemley. "Charity Signs for Herself: Gender and the Withdrawal of Black Women from Field Labor, Alabama, 1865-1876." Ph.D. diss., University of California, Irvine, 1991.

Moore, Ross H. "Social and Economic Conditions During Reconstruction." Ph.D. diss., Duke University, 1937.

Olds, Madelin Joan. "The Rape Complex in the Postbellum South." Ph.D. diss., Carnegie-Mellon University, 1989.

Owens, Nora Estelle. "Presidential Reconstruction in Texas: A Case Study." Ph.D. diss., Auburn University, 1983.

Salem, Dorothy C. "To Better Our World: Black Women in Organized Reform, 1890-1920." Ph.D. diss., Kent State University, 1986.

Schwalm, Leslie Ann. "The Meaning of Freedom: African—American Women and Their Transition From Slavery to Freedom in Low Country South Carolina." Ph.D. diss., The University of Wisconsin-Madison, 1991.

Shaw, Stephanie. "Black Women in White Collars: A Social History of Lower Level Professional Black Women Workers, 1870-1954." Ph.D. diss., Ohio State University, 1986.

Shook, Robert W. "Federal Occupation and Administration of Texas,1865-1870." Ph.D. diss., North Texas State University, 1970.

Smith, Susan Lynn. "The Black Woman's Club Movement: Self—Improvement and Sisterhood." Master's Thesis, University of Wisconsin, 1986.

Stanley, Jeanie R. "Cultural Politics in an East Texas Community." Ph.D. diss., University of Texas, 1981.

Thompson, Esther Lane. "The Influence of the Freedmen's Bureau on the Education of the Negro in Texas." Thesis, Texas Southern University, 1956.

Weiner, Marli Frances. "Plantation Mistress, Female Slave: Gender, Race, and South Carolina Women, 1830-1880." Ph.D. diss., University of Rochester, 1985.

White, Michael Allen. "History of Education in Texas, 1860-1884." Ed.D. diss., Baylor University, 1962.

INDEX

LaVonne Jackson Leslie, Ph.D.

Women 5, 9, 10, 11, 12, 13, 14,
        33, 59, 60, 73, 77, 84, 89,
        100, 104, 106, 107, 110,
        111, 119, 131, 136, 137,
        138, 139, 140, 141, 142,
        143, 144, 145, 146, 147,
        148, 149, 150, 151, 152,
        153, 154, 155, 156, 157,
        158, 159, 160, 161, 162,
        163, 164, 165, 166, 167,
        169, 170, 171, 172, 173,
        174, 175, 176, 177, 178,
        179, 180, 181, 182

LaVonne Leslie Jackson is an Associate Professor at Howard University in the Department of Afro-American Studies. She has an earned doctorate in United States History with specialization in 19th Century History, African Studies, and Women History. She is the author of numerous essays, articles, books and encyclopedia entries about the Black experience and women in America. She resides in Washington, DC.

Freedom After Slavery: The Black Experience and the Freedmen's Bureau in Texas, provides a historical study of slavery and emancipation in Texas with emphasis on the lives of slaves and freedpeople during their transition to freedom. It reveals a first hand account of the experiences of slaves as they refashion their lives in the midst of formidable challenges. Though services of the Freedmen's Bureau, freed slaves in Texas made significant adjustments in their communities.